Contents

INTERNAL PUBLIC KEY INFRASTRUCTURE (SETUP MANUAL) 3

STEP 1: INSTALLATION OF THE UAT ROOT CERTIFICATE AUTHORITY 4

STEP 2: INSTALLATION OF THE UAT SUBORDINATE CERTIFICATE AUTHORITY 44

STEP 3: PUBLISH ROOT AND INTERMEDIATE CERTIFICATE VIA GROUP POLICY.. 121

STEP 4: ISSUING COMPUTER (MACHINE) CERTIFICATES THROUGHOUT THE DOMAIN VIA THE AUTOMATIC CERTIFICATE REQUEST 140

STEP 5: CREATING AND DEPLOYING REMOTE DESKTOP PROTOCOL CERTIFICATES USING GROUP POLICY OBJECTS (GPO) 149

STEP 6: CONFIGURING THE CERTIFICATE THAT IS TO BE USED FOR REMOTE DESKTOP PROTOCOL USING A GROUP POLICY OBJECT (GPO) 176

STEP 7: CONFIGURING USER CERTIFICATES VIA A GROUP POLICY OBJECT (GPO) 182

 Microsoft    Active Directory

INTERNAL PUBLIC KEY INFRASTRUCTURE (SETUP MANUAL)

__UAT Root Certificate Authority__
TTZSECWINAPP.UAT.UBCRDB.COM
172.31.4.136

__UAT Intermediate Certificate Authority__
UAT-ADS.UAT.UBCRDB.COM
172.31.1.150

UAT Domain Digital Certificates

 **Microsoft**    Active Directory

STEP 1: INSTALLATION OF THE UAT ROOT CERTIFICATE AUTHORITY

Test Server: TTZSECWINAPP.UAT.UBCRDB.COM
IP Address: 172.31.4.136

In the Server Manager select Manage → Add Roles and Features

Click Next

4

 Microsoft

 Active Directory

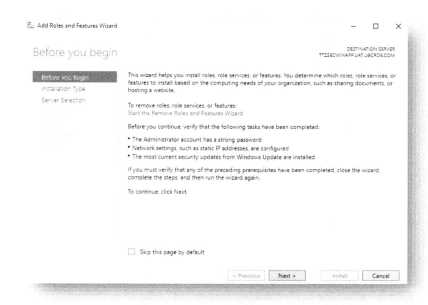

Select the Role-based or feature-based installation type and click Next

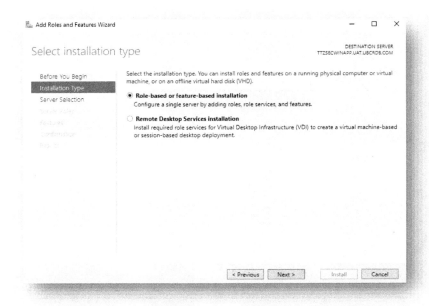

Add Roles and Features Wizard   — ☐ ✕

Select installation type   DESTINATION SERVER
                                                      TTZSECWINAPP.UAT.UBCRDB.COM

Before You Begin   Select the installation type. You can install roles and features on a running physical computer or virtual
                          machine, or on an offline virtual hard disk (VHD).
Installation Type
Server Selection   ● **Role-based or feature-based installation**
                            Configure a single server by adding roles, role services, and features.

                          ○ **Remote Desktop Services installation**
                            Install required role services for Virtual Desktop Infrastructure (VDI) to create a virtual machine-based
                            or session-based desktop deployment.

                          < Previous   Next >   Install   Cancel

Select a server from the server pool and Click Next

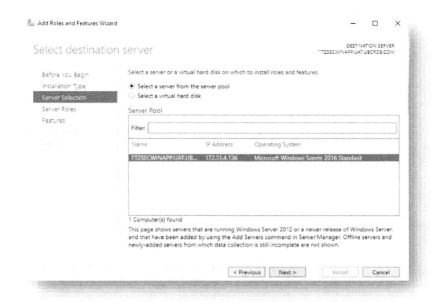

Check the Active Directory Certificate Services Server Role Checkbox.

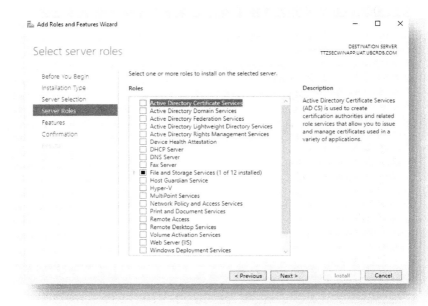

Select the Add Features button

📑 Add Roles and Features Wizard   ✕

Add features that are required for Active Directory Certificate Services?

The following tools are required to manage this feature, but do not have to be installed on the same server.

> ◢ Remote Server Administration Tools
>> ◢ Role Administration Tools
>>> ◢ Active Directory Certificate Services Tools
>>>> [Tools] Certification Authority Management Tools

☑ Include management tools (if applicable)

                                        [Add Features]   [Cancel]

Once the Checkbox is checked click on Next

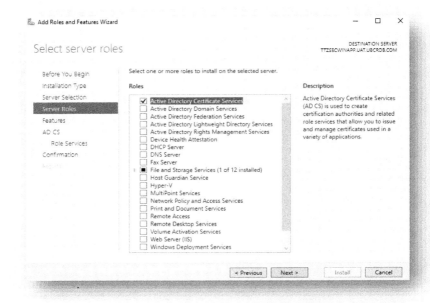

Click Next on the Features selection window

Add Roles and Features Wizard

Select features

DESTINATION SERVER
TTZSECWINAPP.UAT.UBCRDB.COM

Before You Begin
Installation Type
Server Selection
Server Roles
Features
AD CS
    Role Services
Confirmation

Select one or more features to install on the selected server.

Features

- [ ] .NET Framework 3.5 Features
- [■] .NET Framework 4.6 Features (2 of 7 installed)
- [ ] Background Intelligent Transfer Service (BITS)
- [✓] BitLocker Drive Encryption (Installed)
- [ ] BitLocker Network Unlock
- [ ] BranchCache
- [ ] Client for NFS
- [ ] Containers
- [ ] Data Center Bridging
- [ ] Direct Play
- [✓] Enhanced Storage (Installed)
- [ ] Failover Clustering
- [ ] Group Policy Management
- [ ] I/O Quality of Service
- [ ] IIS Hostable Web Core
- [ ] Internet Printing Client
- [ ] IP Address Management (IPAM) Server
- [ ] iSNS Server service
- [ ] LPR Port Monitor

Description

.NET Framework 3.5 combines the power of the .NET Framework 2.0 APIs with new technologies for building applications that offer appealing user interfaces, protect your customers' personal identity information, enable seamless and secure communication, and provide the ability to model a range of business processes.

< Previous   Next >   Install   Cancel

Click Next

Select the Certificate Authority Role Service and click Next

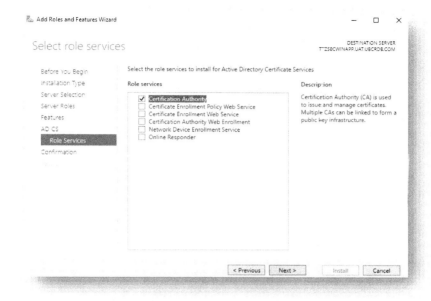

Select Install

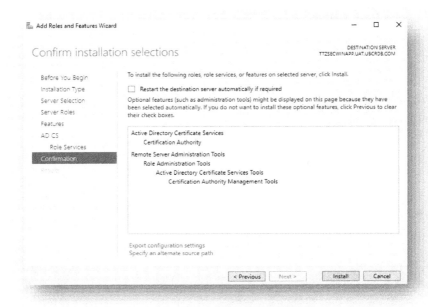

Allow the installer to run to completion

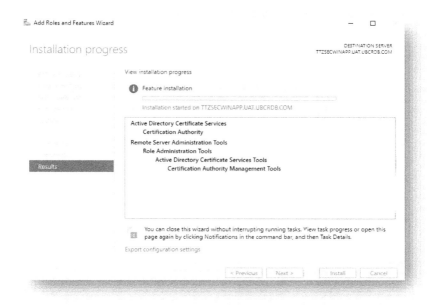

Note that configuration is required and Close the installer.

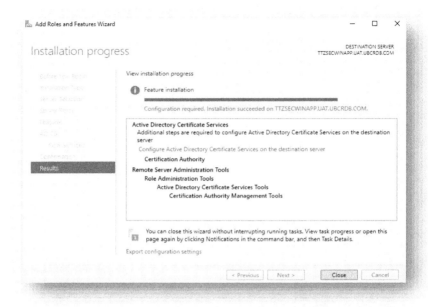

On the Server Manager, under the Post-deployment Configuration Tab, select Configure Active Directory Certificate Services on the destination server.

Specify the credentials to configure role services and select Next.

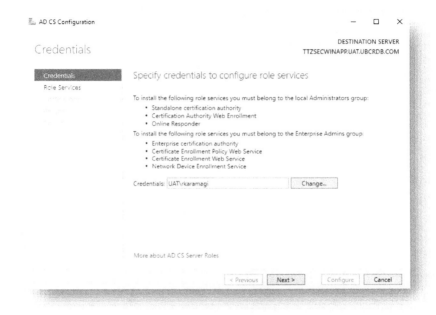

Check the Certification Authority check box and click Next.

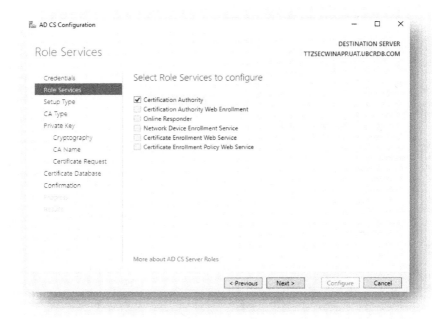

Select the standalone CA setup type and click Next.

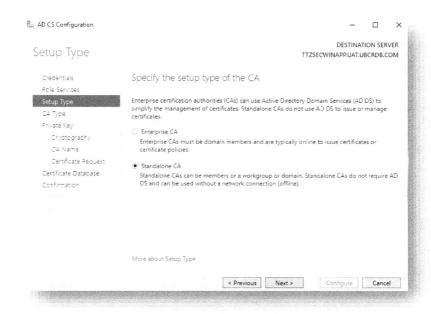

Select the Root CA type and click Next.

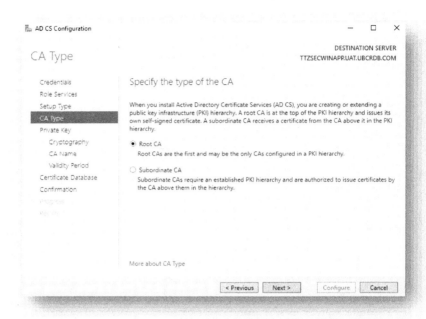

Select create a new private key

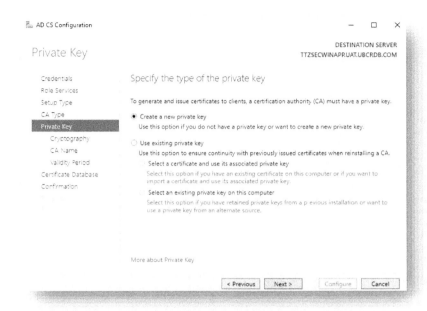

Select the RSA#Microsoft Software Key Storage Provider with a Key length of 4096 bits and a hash algorithm of SHA512.

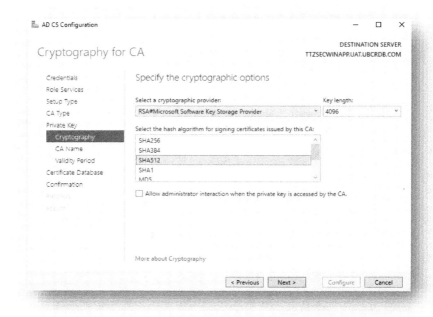

Set a proper common name according to the naming standard

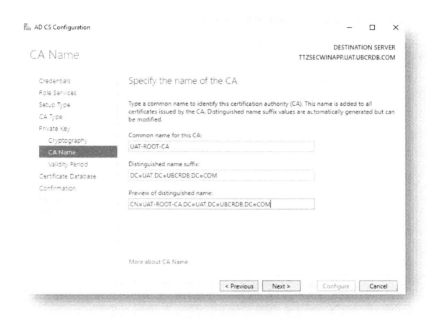

We select a validity period of 50 years for our undisturbed Root
Certification Authority and click on Next

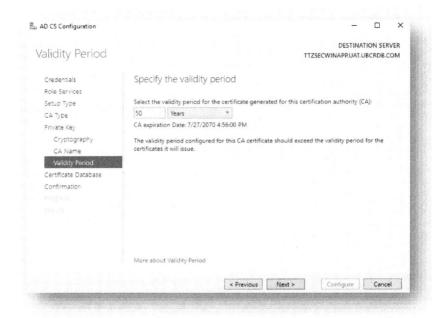

Select the default certificate database and log location

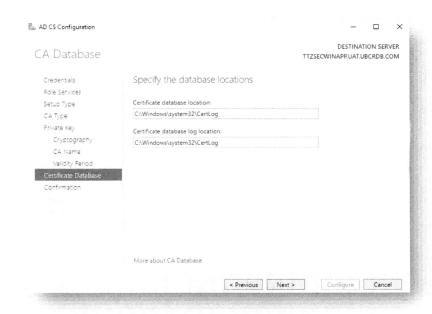

Click on the Configure button, to apply the configuration settings

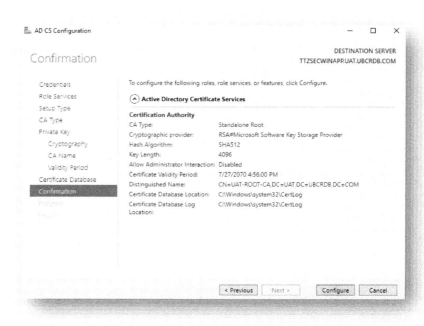

Once the Configuration succeeds, Close the window.

The Post-deployment Configuration is complete

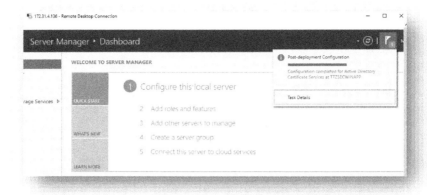

Select the Tools Tab → Certification Authority

Validate the installation is successful

There are two distribution points of information that are critical and we need to make them independent of any physical box. We want to make it in such a way that any subordinate CA can get this information.

(i) **Certificate Revocation List Distribution Point (CDP)** – A CRL Distribution Point (CDP) is a certificate extension that points to a location of a CRL. From the specified location, the Policy Server can retrieve the CRL and can confirm which certificates are revoked. A CDP extension can specify several sources to locate a CRL. Each source contains all the information to locate a CRL.

(ii) **Authority Information Access Role (AIA)** – Is a special extension in SSL certificates that contains information about the issuer of the certificate. This extension helps fetch intermediate certificates from the issuing certification authority.

Right Click on the Server and Select Properties

Click on the Extensions Tab.
Select the CRL Distribution Point (CDP) extension.
Click on the Add button to specify locations from which users can obtain a certificate revocation list (CRL).

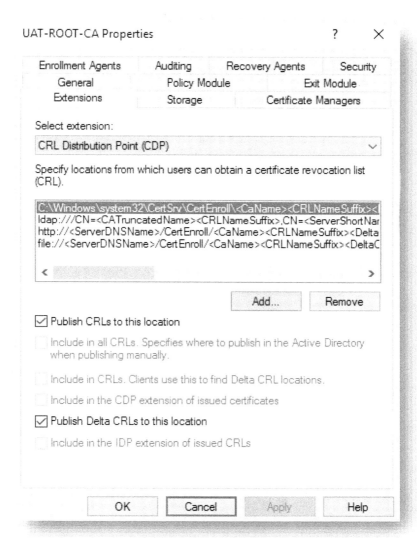

Add the location
http://pki.uat.ubcrdb.com/cdp/<CaName><CRLNameSuffix>.crl

Type the location _http://pki.uat.ubcrdb.com/cdp/_ → select the <CAName> variable and click Insert

On the location _http://pki.uat.ubcrdb.com/cdp/<CAName>_ → select the <CRLNameSuffix> variable and click Insert

Add the extension .crl to the location
http://pki.uat.ubcrdb.com/cdp/<CaName><CRLNameSuffix> and click
OK

Microsoft

Active Directory

Add Location   ✕

A location can be any valid URL or path. Enter an HTTP, LDAP, file address, or enter a UNC or local path. To insert a variable into the URL or path, select the variable below and click Insert.

Location:

```
http://pki.uat.ubcrdb.com/cdp/<CaName><CRLNameSuffix>.crl|
```

Variable:

```
<CRLNameSuffix>                                    ∨        Insert
```

Description of selected variable:

```
Used in URLs and paths for the CRL Distribution Points extension
Appends a suffix to distinguish the CRL file name
Example location: http://<ServerName>/CertEnroll/<CaName><CRLNameSu
```

‹   ›

                                           OK   Cancel

Click on the location just added and make sure you check the box "Include in the CDP extension of issued certificates" then click Apply.

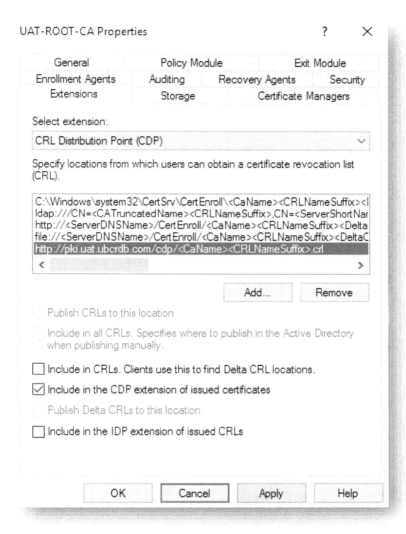

Restart Active Directory Certificate Services for the changes to take effect.

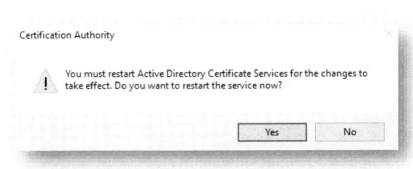

Select the Authority Information Access (AIA) extension and select Add

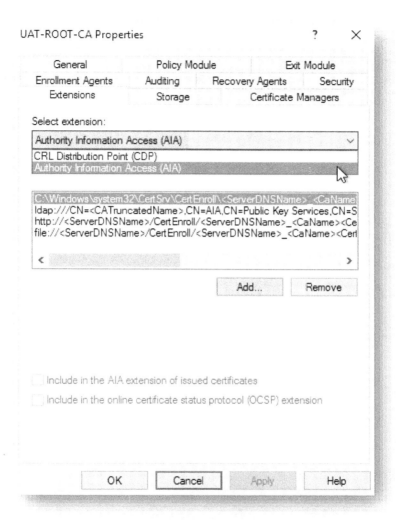

Add the location
http://pki.uat.ubcrdb.com/aia/<CaName><CertificateName>.crt

Type the location *http://pki.uat.ubcrdb.com/aia/* → select the
<CAName> variable and click Insert

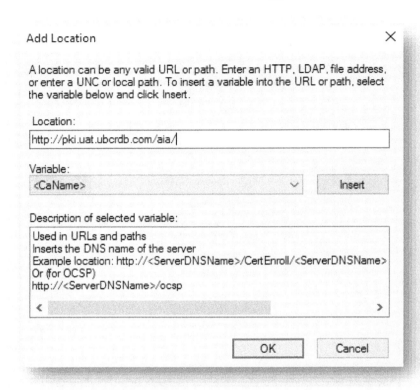

Add Location   ✕

A location can be any valid URL or path. Enter an HTTP, LDAP, file address, or enter a UNC or local path. To insert a variable into the URL or path, select the variable below and click Insert.

Location:

http://pki.uat.ubcrdb.com/aia/

Variable:

<CaName>   ⌄   [Insert]

Description of selected variable:

Used in URLs and paths
Inserts the DNS name of the server
Example location: http://<ServerDNSName>/CertEnroll/<ServerDNSName>
Or (for OCSP)
http://<ServerDNSName>/ocsp

‹   ›

[OK]   [Cancel]

On the location *http://pki.uat.ubcrdb.com/aia/<CAName>* → select the < CertificateName> variable and click Insert

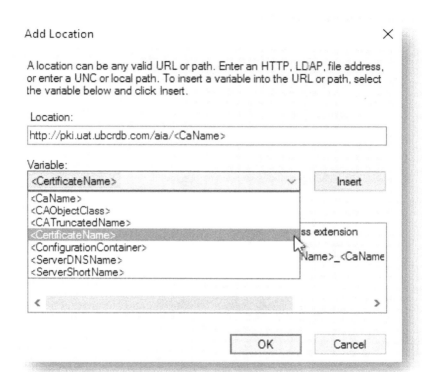

Add the extension .crt to the location
http://pki.uat.ubcrdb.com/aia/<CaName><CertificateName> and click
OK

Add Location   ✕

A location can be any valid URL or path. Enter an HTTP, LDAP, file address,
or enter a UNC or local path. To insert a variable into the URL or path, select
the variable below and click Insert.

Location:

| http://pki.uat.ubcrdb.com/aia/<CaName><CertificateName>.crt| |

Variable:

| <CertificateName>   ⌄ | | Insert |

Description of selected variable:

Used in URLs and paths for the Authority Information Access extension
Appends a suffix to distinguish the certificate file name
Example location: file://<ServerName>/CertEnroll/<ServerName>_<CaName

‹ ▭▭▭▭▭▭▭▭▭▭▭▭▭▭▭▭▭▭   ›

| OK | Cancel |

Click on the location just added and make sure you check the box
"Include in the AIA extension of issued certificates" then click Apply.

 Microsoft    Active Directory

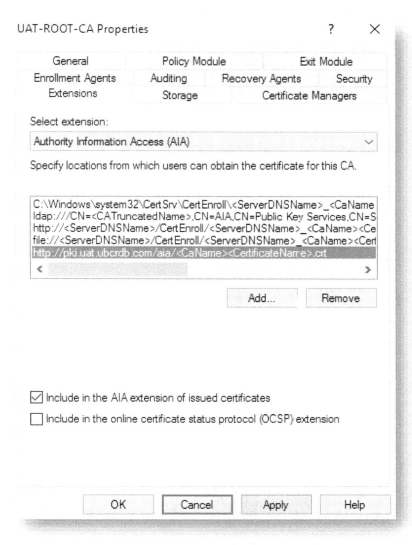

Restart Active Directory Certificate Services for the changes to take effect.

We manually publish the current Certificate Revocation List by Right-clicking on the Revoked Certificates → selecting All Tasks → Publish

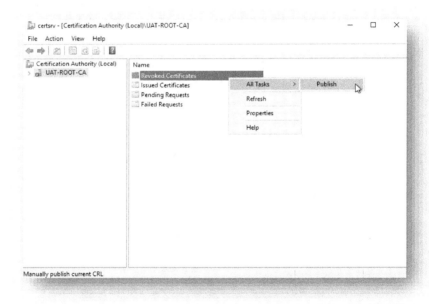

Click OK to publish the Certificate Revocation List (CRL)

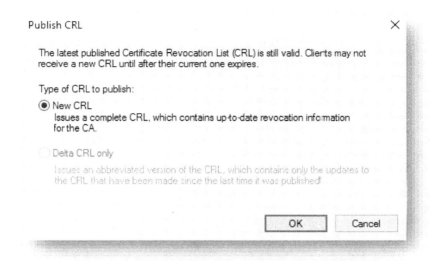

Publish CRL   ✕

The latest published Certificate Revocation List (CRL) is still valid. Clients may not receive a new CRL until after their current one expires.

Type of CRL to publish:

⦿ New CRL
Issues a complete CRL, which contains up-to-date revocation information for the CA.

◯ Delta CRL only
Issues an abbreviated version of the CRL, which contains only the updates to the CRL that have been made since the last time it was published.

[OK]   [Cancel]

Navigate to the directory location C:\Windows\System32\CertSrv\CertEnroll to obtain the Root Security Certificate and the newly published Certificate Revocation List. These files shall be used on the subordinate certificate authority server.

STEP 2: INSTALLATION OF THE UAT SUBORDINATE CERTIFICATE AUTHORITY

Select Manage → Add Roles and Features on the Subordinate Certificate Authority Server (172.31.1.150)

Note that we shall install an Enterprise Subordinate Certificate Authority on this server so it is compulsory that Active Directory Domain Services (AD DS) is installed on the server as well.

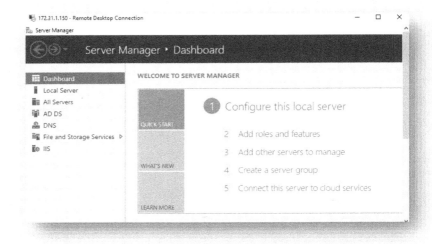

Click Next to proceed with the Wizard

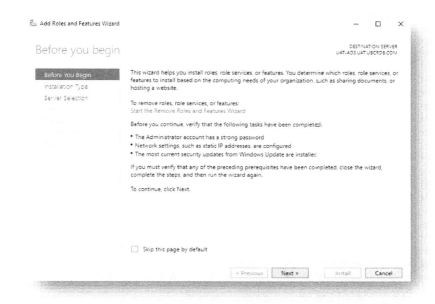

Select the Role-based or feature-based installation and Click Next

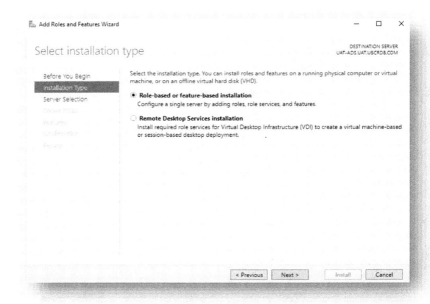

Select the server from the server pool and click on the Next button

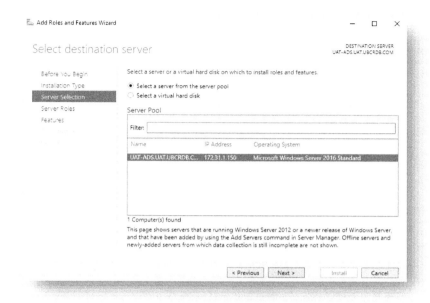

Select the Active Directory Certificate Services role to install on the selected server.

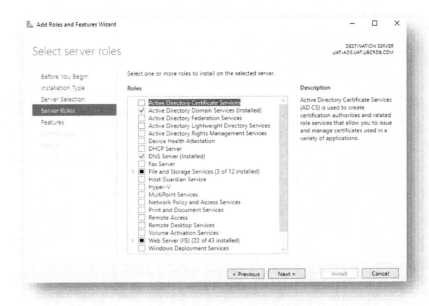

Check the Include management tools (if applicable) check box and click on the Add Features button.

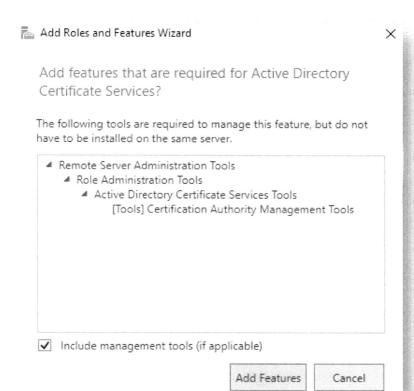

Once the Active Directory Certificate checkbox is checked, click on the Next button.

You may settle with the default features and click on the Next button.

The dialog gives a brief explanation on Active Directory Certificate Services. Click the Next button

Select All the features that you want to install and click Next.

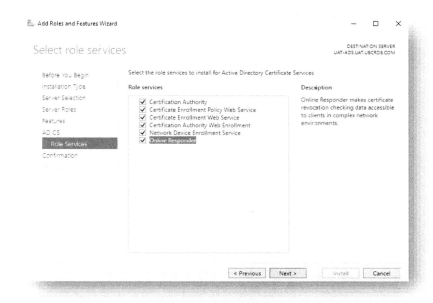

Click on the Install button.

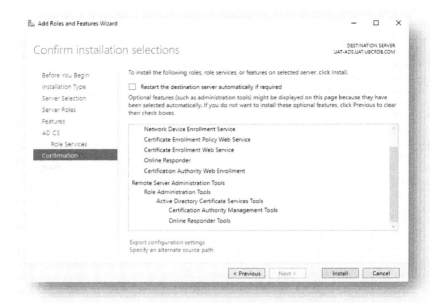

Wait for the installation to complete.

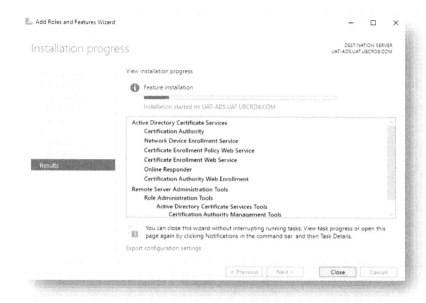

Once the installation has succeeded click on the Close button. Notice that a Configuration is still required.

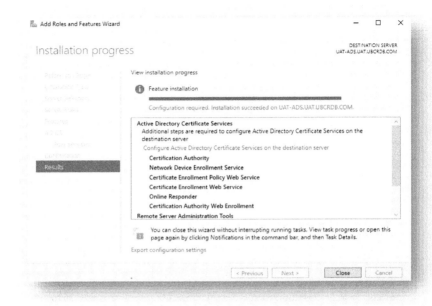

Click on the label "Configure Active Directory Certificate Services on the Destination Server"

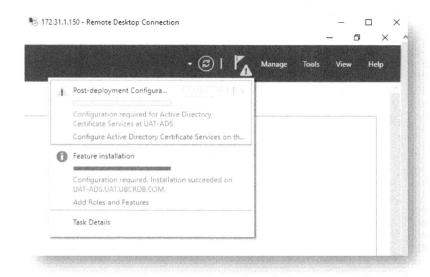

Supply appropriate credentials and click the Next button.

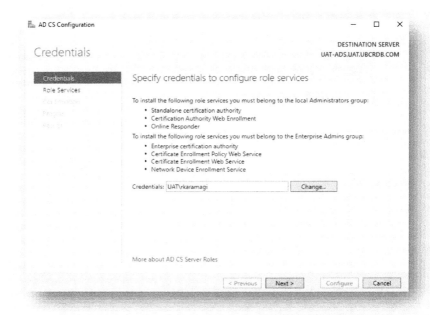

Select the Role services to configure and click the Next button.

 Microsoft

 Active Directory

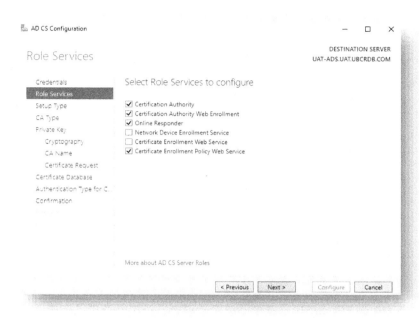

Note that the Network Device Enrollment Service and the Certificate Enrollment Web Service cannot be installed before the setting up the Certificate Authority.

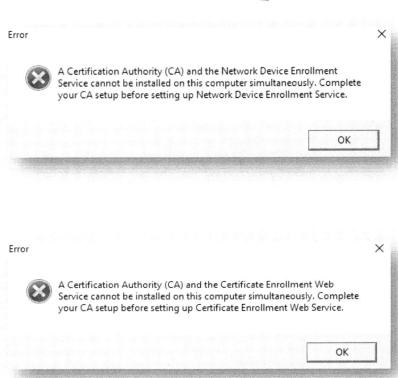

Error ✕

A Certification Authority (CA) and the Network Device Enrollment
Service cannot be installed on this computer simultaneously. Complete
your CA setup before setting up Network Device Enrollment Service.

OK

Error ✕

A Certification Authority (CA) and the Certificate Enrollment Web
Service cannot be installed on this computer simultaneously. Complete
your CA setup before setting up Certificate Enrollment Web Service.

OK

Select the Enterprise CA radio button and then click on the Next button.

 Microsoft

 Active Directory

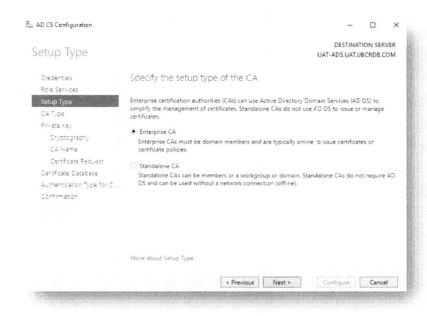

Select the Subordinate CA radio button and then click the Next button.

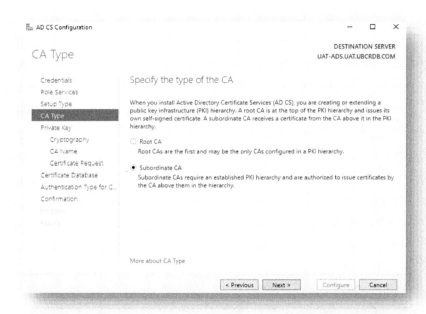

Select the Create a new private key radio button and click Next.

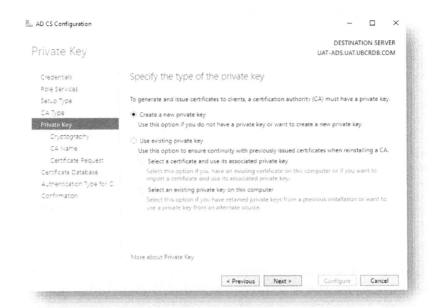

Select the following:

Cryptographic provider: RSA#Microsoft Software Key Storage Provider;

Key length: 4096;

Hash algorithm for signing certificates issued by this CA: SHA512;

then click the Next button

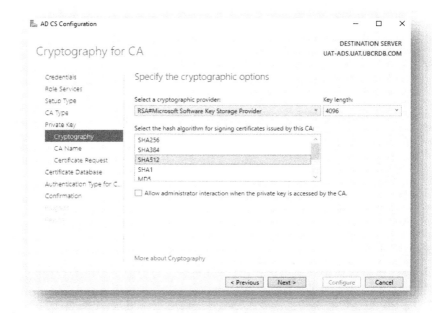

Type the common name for this CA:
UAT-INTERMEDIATE-CA
then click the Next button

AD CS Configuration — □ ×

CA Name

DESTINATION SERVER
UAT-ADS.UAT.UBCRDB.COM

Credentials
Role Services
Setup Type
CA Type
Private Key
Cryptography
CA Name
Certificate Request
Certificate Database
Authentication Type for C...
Confirmation

Specify the name of the CA

Type a common name to identify this certification authority (CA). This name is added to all
certificates issued by the CA. Distinguished name suffix values are automatically generated but can
be modified.

Common name for this CA:

UAT-INTERMEDIATE-CA

Distinguished name suffix:

DC=UAT,DC=UBCRDB,DC=COM

Preview of distinguished name:

CN=UAT-INTERMEDIATE-CA,DC=UAT,DC=UBCRDB,DC=COM

More about CA Name

< Previous   Next >   Configure   Cancel

Click on the radio button "Save a certificate request to file on the target machine:"
You may opt for the default file name and click the Next button.

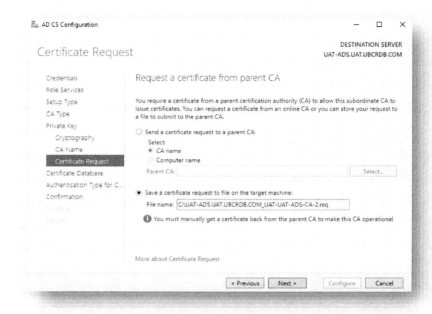

You may leave the default database and database log location as C:\WINDOWS\system32\CertLog and then click the Next button.

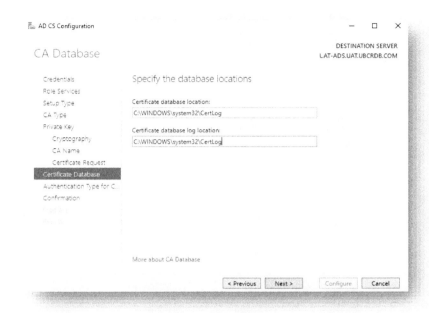

Select the Windows integrated authentication and then click the Next button.

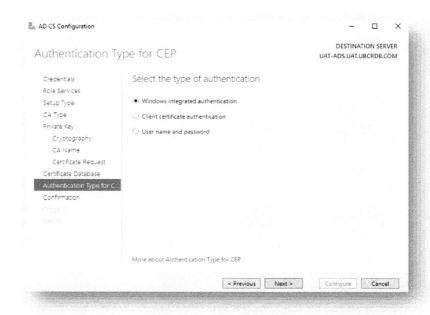

Click the Configure button to configure the roles, role services and features.

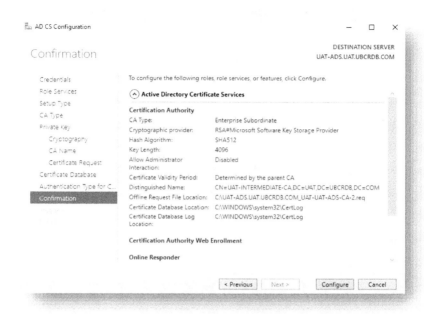

Wait for the configuration of the Active Directory Certificate Services to complete

Click the Close button once the Services have completed.

In the C:/ directory, you will find the certificate signing request (CSR) file as below:-

UAT-ADS.UAT.UBCRDB.COM_UAT-UAT-ADS-CA-2.req

Copy this file from the UAT Intermediate Certificate Authority Server (172.31.1.150) to the UAT Root Certificate Authority Server (172.31.4.136)

Open the Certificate Authority Manager.
Right Click on the Server and select All Tasks → Submit new request

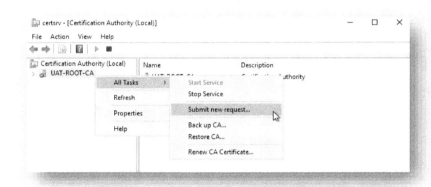

Select the request file and click Open.

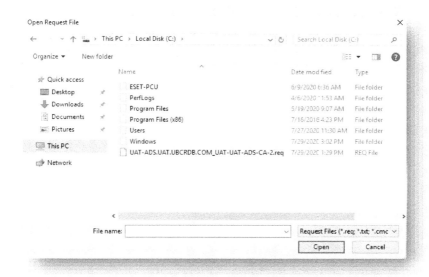

Notice the Certificate Signing Request in the Pending Requests Folder

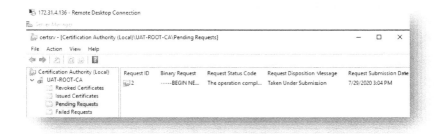

Right Click the Certificate Signing Request and select All Tasks → Issue

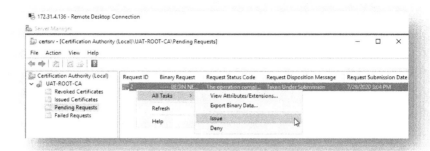

Once the certificate signing request (CSR) is issued the Pending Requests Folder will be cleared of the CSR. In our practical case the window will display "There are no items to show in this view."

The certificate will move to the Issued Certificates folder.

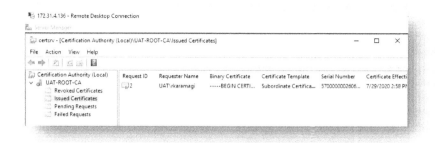

Double-click the certificate to see its contents

 Microsoft

 Active Directory

Certificate   ✕

General   Details   Certification Path

Certificate Information

This certificate is intended for the following purpose(s):
- All application policies

Issued to: UAT-INTERMEDIATE-CA

Issued by: UAT-ROOT-CA

Valid from   7/29/2020 **to** 7/29/2021

Issuer Statement

OK

 Microsoft    Active Directory

The certification path shows that the UAT-INTERMEDIATE-CA was signed by the UAT-ROOT-CA.

Certificate   ✕

General   Details   Certification Path

Certification path

```
UAT-ROOT-CA
    UAT-INTERMEDIATE-CA
```

[View Certificate]

Certificate status:

This certificate is OK.|

[OK]

In the Details Tab, click on the Copy to File... button.

Certificate ✕

General   Details   Certification Path

Show: <All>   ⌄

Field	Value	
Version	V3	
Serial number	57 00 00 00 02 60 60 e4 66 54...	
Signature algorithm	sha512RSA	
Signature hash algorithm	sha512	
Issuer	UAT-ROOT-CA, UAT, UBCRDB...	
Valid from	Wednesday, July 29, 2020 2:...	
Valid to	Thursday, July 29, 2021 3:08:...	
Subject	UAT-INTERMEDIATE-CA, UAT	

Edit Properties...   Copy to File...

OK

The Certificate Export Wizard window shall pop up. Click on the Next button.

Select the Cryptographic Message Syntax Standard – PKCS #7 Certificates (.P7B) radio button and check the "Include all certificates in the certification path if possible" checkbox and then click the Next button.

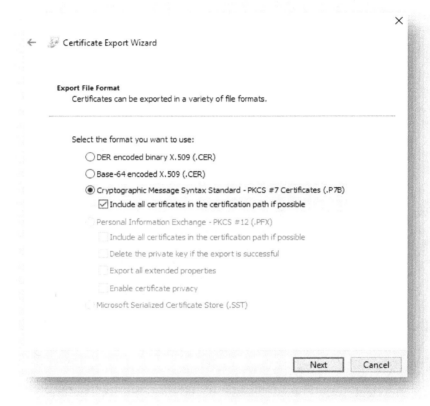

Provide the File name for the certificate you are exporting and click the Next button.

Click on the Finish button to complete the Certificate Export.

A dialog will appear showing "The export was successful". Click the OK button.

Copy the Root Certificate Authority Certificate (TTZSECWINAPP.UAT.UBCRDB.COM_UAT-ROOT-CA.crt) and the Certificate Revocation List file (UAT-ROOT-CA.crl) from C:\Windows\System32\CertSrv\CertEnroll to the Intermediate Certificate Authority Server at 172.31.1.150

Similarly, copy the Intermediate Certificate Authority Certificate (Intermediate-CA-Certificate.p7b) issued by the Root Certificate Authority (172.31.4.136) to the Intermediate Certif cate Authority Server at 172.31.1.150

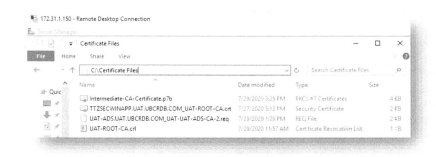

Install the Root Certificate Authority Certificate (TTZSECWINAPP.UAT.UBCRDB.COM_UAT-ROOT-CA.crt)

Double-click on the certificate file. In the General Tab select the "Install Certificate" button

Select the Local Machine Store Location and click Next.

Select the "Place all certificates in the following store" option and click on the Browse button.

 Active Directory

Select the "Trusted Root Certification Authorities" store and click on the OK button.

Click on the Next button.

Click on the Finish button.

Click the OK button, once the import is successful.

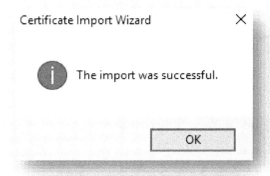

Open the Certification Authority Explorer in your Intermediate CA. Right-click the CA, select All Tasks → Install CA Certificate...

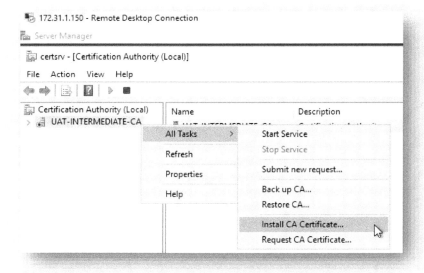

Browse to the folder where the Intermediate CA certificate is stored and select it, then click the Open button.

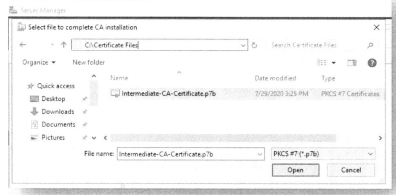

Right-click on the Certificate Authority → select All Tasks → Start Service

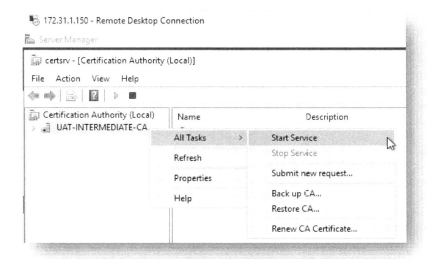

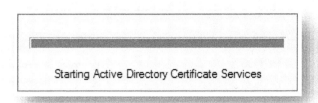

The Certificate Authority services will start. A green tick icon will display that it has started.

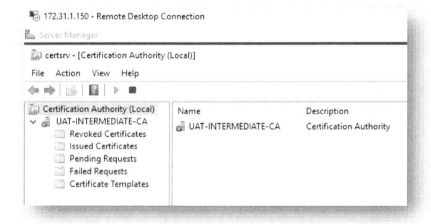

To publish the Certificate Revocation List, navigate to the directory C:\inetpub\wwwroot

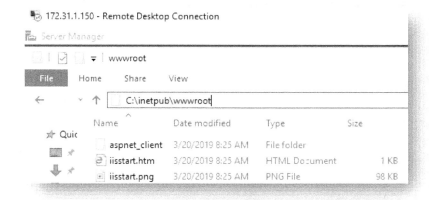

Create the folder pki.

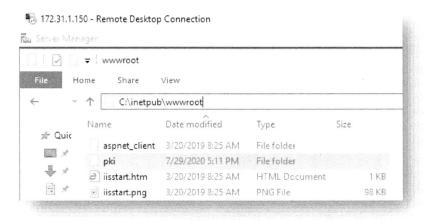

Create the folders aia and cdp in the pki folder.

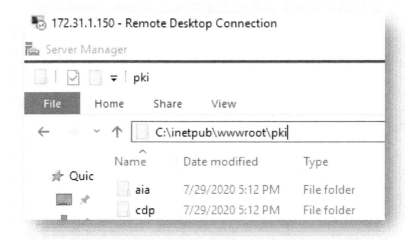

Right-click the pki folder and select Properties.

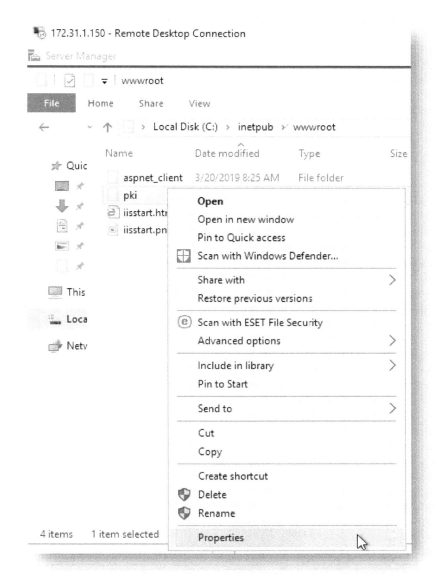

In the Security Tab click Edit.

95

 **Microsoft**

 Active Directory

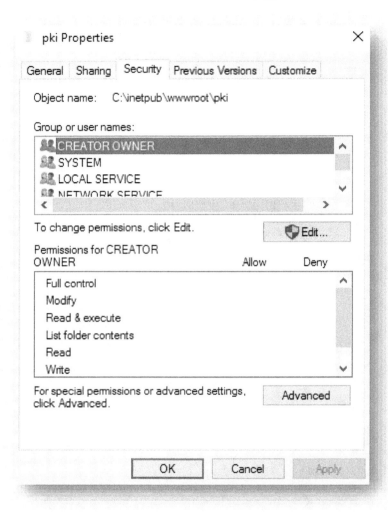

pki Properties ☐ ✕

General Sharing Security Previous Versions Customize

Object name: C:\inetpub\wwwroot\pki

Group or user names:

👥 CREATOR OWNER
👥 SYSTEM
👥 LOCAL SERVICE
👥 NETWORK SERVICE

To change permissions, click Edit.   🛡 Edit...

Permissions for CREATOR
OWNER   Allow   Deny

Full control		
Modify		
Read & execute		
List folder contents		
Read		
Write		

For special permissions or advanced settings,   Advanced
click Advanced.

OK   Cancel   Apply

In the Permissions for pki window select Add.

Permissions for pki   ✕

Security

Object name: C:\inetpub\wwwroot\pki

Group or user names:

👥 CREATOR OWNER
👥 SYSTEM
👥 LOCAL SERVICE
👥 NETWORK SERVICE
👥 Administrators (UAT\Administrators)

[Add...]   [Remove]

Permissions for CREATOR
OWNER   Allow   Deny

	Allow	Deny
Full control	☐	☐
Modify	☐	☐
Read & execute	☐	☐
List folder contents	☐	☐
Read	☐	☐

[OK]   [Cancel]   [Apply]

Enter the "Cert Publishers" and click the OK button.

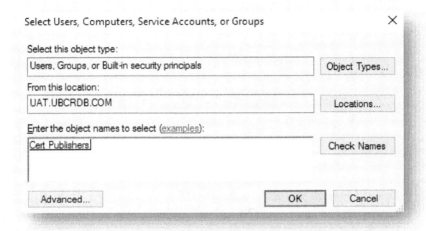

Click the Apply button.

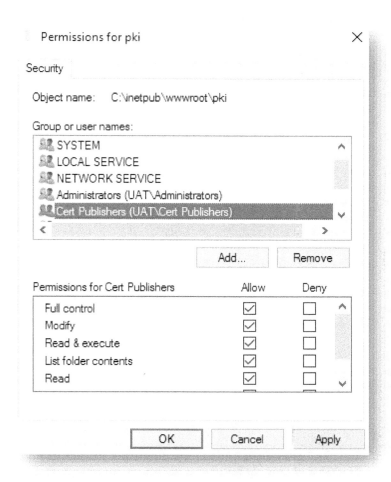

99

Copy the Certificate Revocation List file to C:\inetpub\wwwroot\pki\cdp

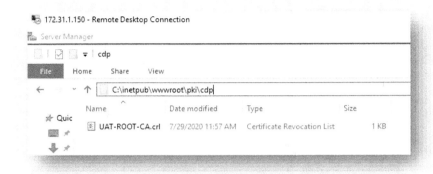

Copy the Root Certificate Authority Certificate to C:\inetpub\wwwroot\pki\aia

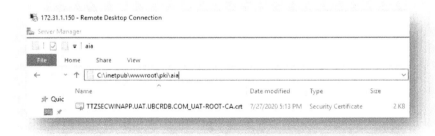

Click on the Tools Tab in the Server Manager and select Internet Information Services (IIS) Manager.

 Microsoft

 Active Directory

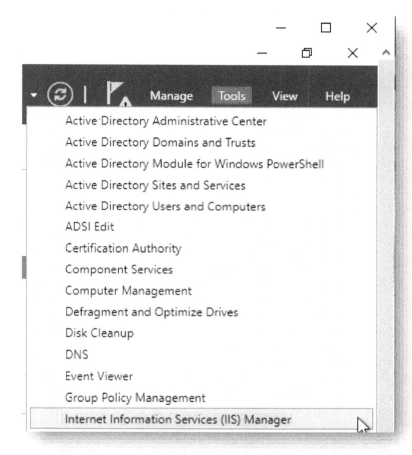

In the Internet Information Services (IIS) Manager, Right-click on the web server and select the Add Website… option.

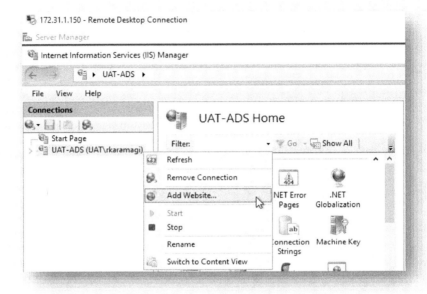

Set the Site name to PKI
Set the Physical Path to C:\inetpub\wwwroot\pki
Set the hostname to pki.uat.ubcrdb.com
Click the Connect as… button

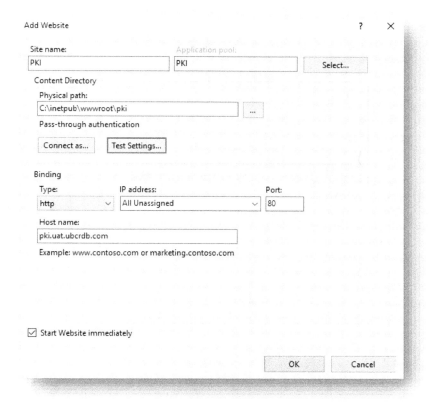

Select the Connect as... button.

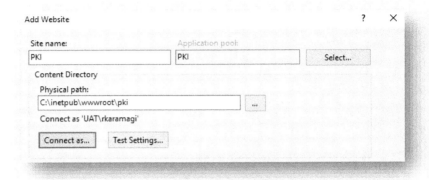

Under the Path credentials, click the Specific user radio option and then click the Set... button.

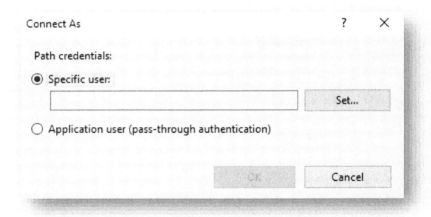

Enter the required credentials for the connection and click the OK button.

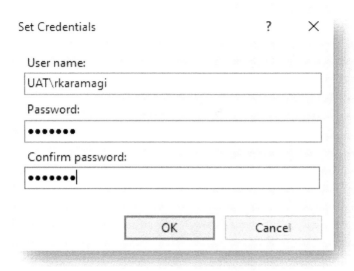

Click the OK button to apply the setting.

Click the Test Settings... button to test the connection settings.

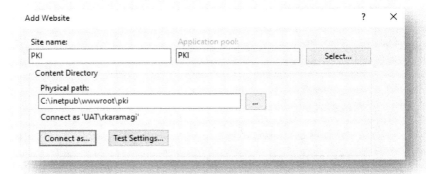

Make sure that the results show a Green Tick icon next to the Authentication and Authorization Test.

Check the "Start Website immediately" checkbox and click the OK button.

In the Internet Information Services (IIS) Manager you will see that the website has started.

Back in the Server Manager click on Tools → DNS.

 Microsoft    Active Directory

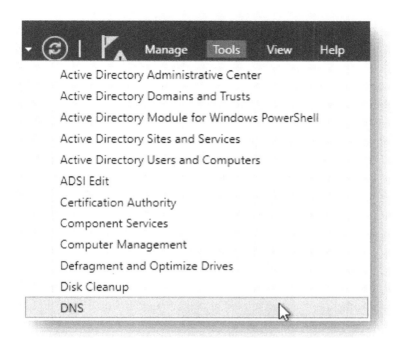

A *forward lookup zone* is a DNS zone in which hostname to IP address relations are stored.
To create a forward lookup zone, once in the DNS Manager, right-click on the Forward Lookup Zone and select New Zone...

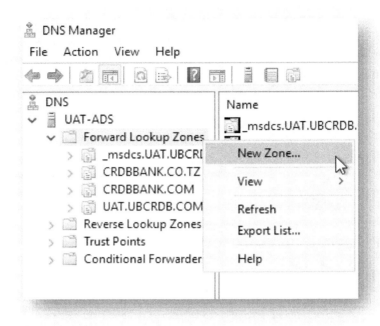

Once the New Zone Wizard opens, click on the Next button.

In the Zone Type window; select the Primary zone radio button and since our DNS server is a writable domain controller with Active Directory Domain Services (AD DS), check the "Store the zone in Active Directory" checkbox and then click the Next button.

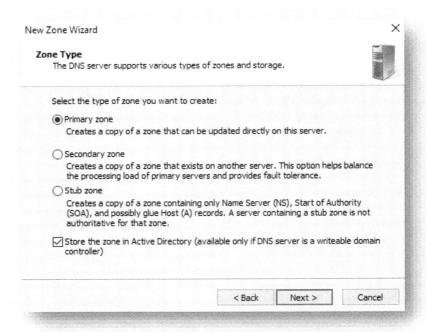

Select the option "To all DNS server running on domain controllers in this forest: UAT.UBCRDB.COM" in the Active Directory Zone Replication Scope window and click the Next button.

New Zone Wizard   ✕

Active Directory Zone Replication Scope
You can select how you want DNS data replicated throughout your network.

Select how you want zone data replicated:

◉ To all DNS servers running on domain controllers in this forest: UAT.UBCRDB.COM

○ To all DNS servers running on domain controllers in this domain: UAT.UBCRDB.COM

○ To all domain controllers in this domain (for Windows 2000 compatibility):
UAT.UBCRDB.COM

○ To all domain controllers specified in the scope of this directory partition:

DomainDnsZones.UAT.UBCRDB.COM

< Back   Next >   Cancel

Type your zone name and click the Next button. For our scope, we have
written it as UAT.UBCRDB.COM

New Zone Wizard   ✕

Zone Name
What is the name of the new zone?

The zone name specifies the portion of the DNS namespace for which this server is
authoritative. It might be your organization's domain name (for example, microsoft.com)
or a portion of the domain name (for example, newzone.microsoft.com). The zone name is
not the name of the DNS server.

Zone name:
| UAT.UBCRDB.COM |

                              < Back   Next >   Cancel

In the Dynamic Update window; select "Allow only secure dynamic
updates" and click the Next button. This is recommended for active
directory.

 Microsoft  Active Directory

New Zone Wizard   ✕

Dynamic Update
You can specify that this DNS zone accepts secure, nonsecure, or no dynamic updates.

Dynamic updates enable DNS client computers to register and dynamically update their resource records with a DNS server whenever changes occur.

Select the type of dynamic updates you want to allow:

◉ Allow only secure dynamic updates (recommended for Active Directory)
   This option is available only for Active Directory-integrated zones

○ Allow both nonsecure and secure dynamic updates
   Dynamic updates of resource records are accepted from any client.
   ⚠ This option is a significant security vulnerability because updates can be accepted from untrusted sources.

○ Do not allow dynamic updates
   Dynamic updates of resource records are not accepted by this zone. You must update these records manually.

[< Back]   [Next >]   [Cancel]

Click the Finish button to Complete the New Zone Wizard.

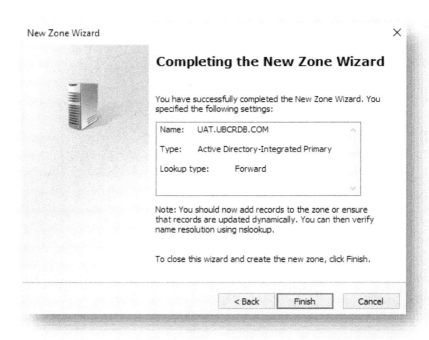

Right-click the UAT.UBCRDB.COM forward lookup zone and select New Host (A or AAAA)...

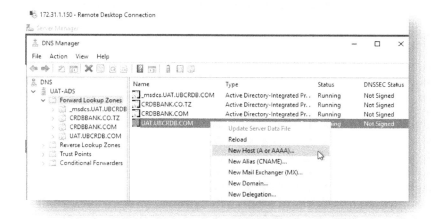

Enter the host name i.e. pki and the IP address of the Web server i.e. 172.31.1.150, then click the Add Host button.

Once the host record pki.UAT.UBCRDB.COM is successfully created click the OK button.

You may navigate to pki.uat.ubcrdb.com in any server within the domain and find the aia and cdp directories available for servers requesting certificate information

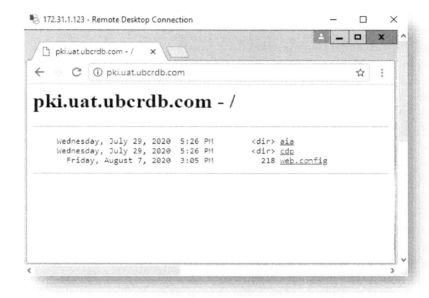

The Authority Information Access (aia) directory has the Root Certificate Authority certificate available for clients.

The Certificate Revocation List (CRL) Distribution Point (CDP) directory contains the Certificate Revocation List available for clients.

STEP 3: PUBLISH ROOT AND INTERMEDIATE CERTIFICATE VIA GROUP POLICY

In the server manager click on the Tools Tab and select the Group Policy Management option.

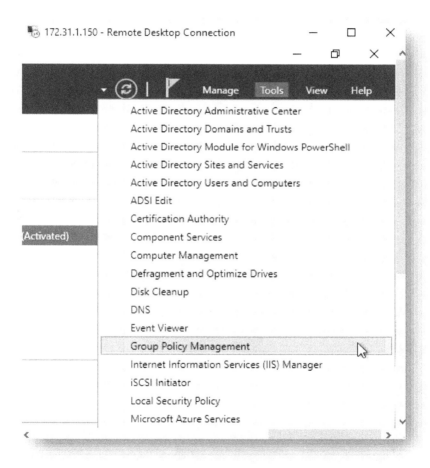

Right-click the domain and select the option "Create a GPO in this domain, and Link it here…"

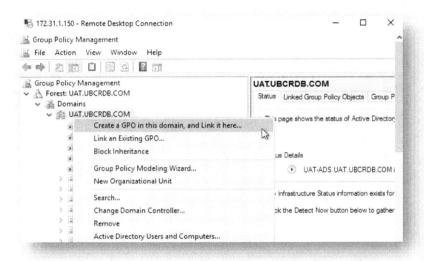

Give a name to the New GPO and click OK. We have given the name as Default Domain Policy.

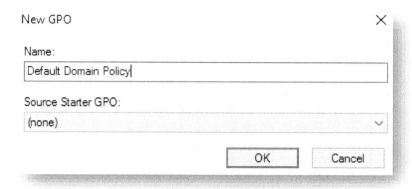

Right-click the Default Domain Policy Group Policy Object (GPO), check the Enforced option and then click the Edit... button.

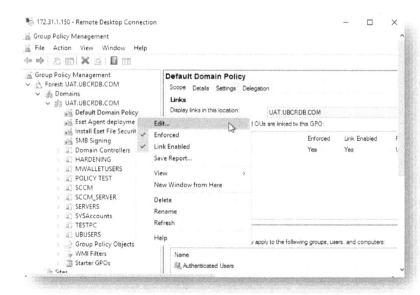

In the Default Domain Policy for [UAT-ADS.UAT.UBCRDB.COM] Policy Navigate to the Computer Configuration → Policies → Windows Settings → Security Settings → Public Key Policies

 Microsoft

 Active Directory

172.31.1.150 - Remote Desktop Connection

Group Policy Management Editor

File   Action   View   Help

Default Domain Policy [UAT-ADS.UAT.UBCRDB.COM] Policy
- Computer Configuration
  - Policies
    - Software Settings
    - Windows Settings
      - Name Resolution Policy
      - Scripts (Startup/Shutdown)
      - Deployed Printers
      - Security Settings
        - Account Policies
        - Local Policies
        - Event Log
        - Restricted Groups
        - System Services
        - Registry
        - File System
        - Wired Network (IEEE 802.3) Policies
        - Windows Firewall with Advanced Security
        - Network List Manager Policies
        - Wireless Network (IEEE 802.11) Policies
        - Public Key Policies
          - Encrypting File System
          - Data Protection
          - BitLocker Drive Encryption
          - BitLocker Drive Encryption Network Unlock Certificate
          - Automatic Certificate Request Settings
          - Trusted Root Certification Authorities
          - Enterprise Trust
          - Intermediate Certification Authorities
          - Trusted Publishers
          - Untrusted Certificates

In the Public Key Policies, right-click the Trusted Root Certification Authorities and select the Import... option.

In the Certificate Import Wizard, click on the Next button.

 Microsoft

 Active Directory

Select the Root Certificate Authority Certificate and click on Open.

127

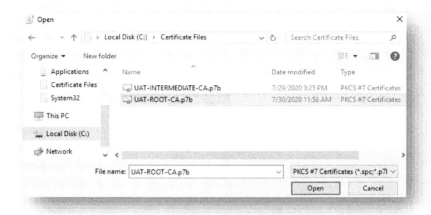

Once the file to import has been inserted in the File name text box, click the Next button.

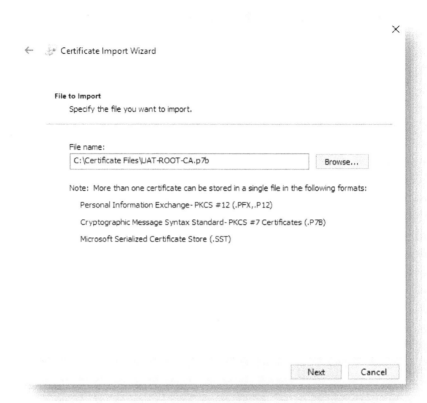

Click the Next button so your certificate is placed in the "Trusted Root Certification Authorities" store.

Click the Finish button to complete the Certificate Import wizard.

Once the import is successful click the OK button.

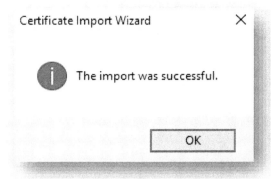

Notice the Root Certification Authority Certificate will appear in your Trusted Root Certification Authorities Group Policy Object (GPO).

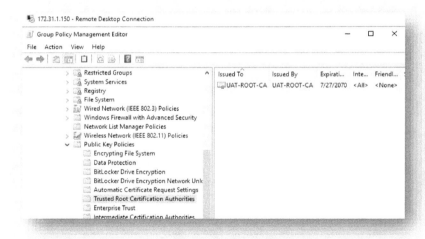

Right-click the Intermediate Certification Authorities and click the Import option.

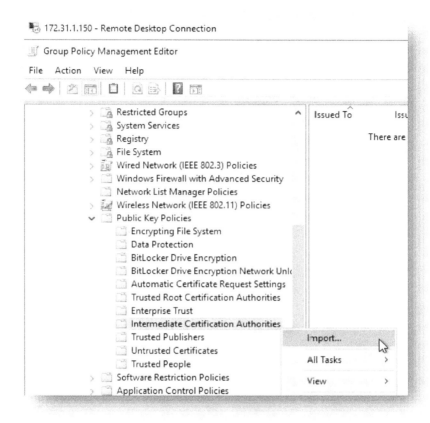

Click the Next button in the Certificate Import Wizard.

Click once on the Intermediate Certification Authority Certificate and click the Open button.

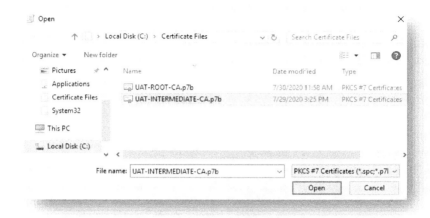

When the certificate to Import appears in the File name text box, click on the Next button.

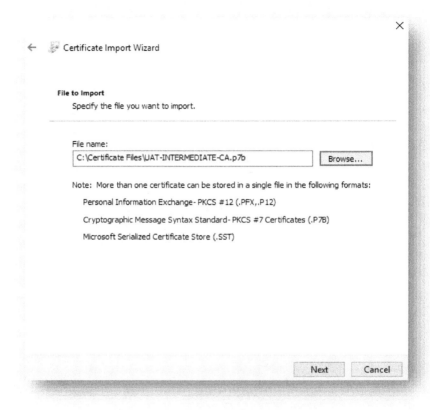

Click the Next button so your certificate is placed in the "Intermediate Certification Authorities" store.

 Microsoft

 Active Directory

Click the Finish button to complete the Certificate Import Wizard.

When the import is successful, click the OK button.

Notice the Intermediate Certification Authority Certificate appear in the window.

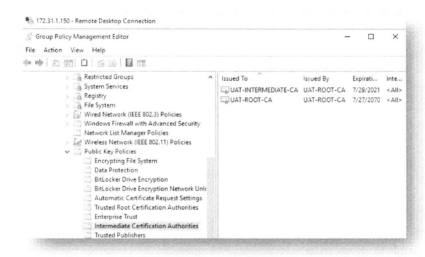

 Microsoft

 Active Directory

STEP 4: ISSUING COMPUTER (MACHINE) CERTIFICATES THROUGHOUT THE DOMAIN VIA THE AUTOMATIC CERTIFICATE REQUEST

In the Server Manager click the Tools tab and select Group Policy Management.

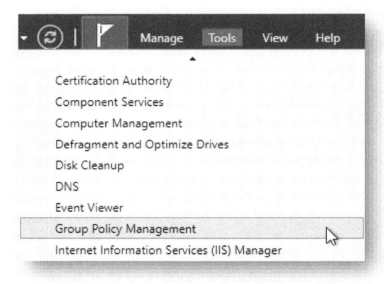

Right-click the Default Domain Policy Group Policy Object created previously and select Edit...

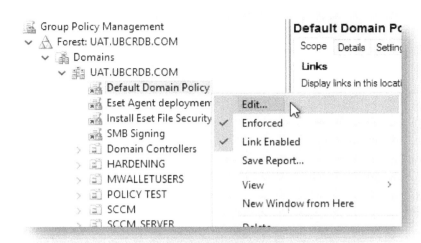

In the Group Policy Management Editor, navigate to Computer Configuration → Windows Settings → Security Settings → Public Key Policies.
Select the "Certificate Services Client – Auto Enrollment" object.

141

 **Microsoft**

 Active Directory

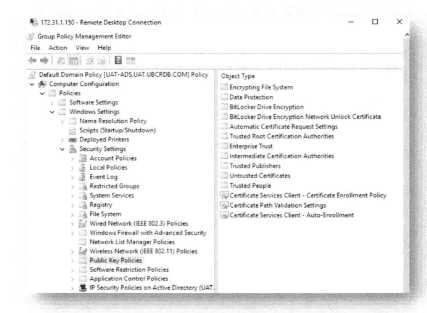

In the Certificate Services Client – Auto Enrollment Properties under the Enrollment Policy Configuration set the following:-

- Configuration Model : Enabled
- Check the checkbox: Renew expired certificates, update pending certificates and remove revoked certificates
- Check the checkbox: Update certificates that use certificate templates

Certificate Services Client - Auto-Enrollment Properties   ?   ✕

Enrollment Policy Configuration

Enroll user and computer certificates automatically

Configuration Model: [Enabled   ⌄]

☑ Renew expired certificates, update pending certificates, and remove revoked certificates

☑ Update certificates that use certificate templates

Log expiry events and show expiry notifications when the percentage of remaining certificate lifetime is

[10 ⬍]   %

Additional stores. Use "," to separate multiple stores. For example: "Store1, Store2, Store3"

[   ]

[OK]   [Cancel]   [Apply]

Return to the Group Policy Management Editor and Navigate to Computer Configuration → Policies → Windows Settings → Security Settings → Public Key Policies
Right-click the "Automatic Certificate Request Settings" and select New → Automatic Certificate Request…

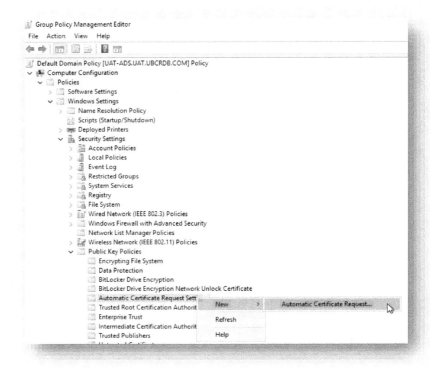

In the Automatic Certificate Request Setup Wizard, click the Next button to continue.

 Microsoft

 Active Directory

Select the Computer Certificate template and then click on the Next button.

Drawback: *The Microsoft® default certificate template settings shall be selected for the issued certificates, which may not have hardened security features.*

Alternatively, you may issue a custom Computer Certificate Template across the domain as in Step 5 and 7.

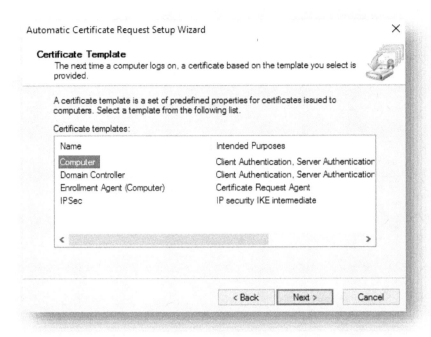

Click the Finish button to complete the Automatic Certificate Request Setup.

Back in the Group Policy Management Editor, in the Computer Configuration → Policies → Windows Settings → Security Settings → Public Key Policies → Automatic Certificate Request; you will see the Computer Certificate.

147

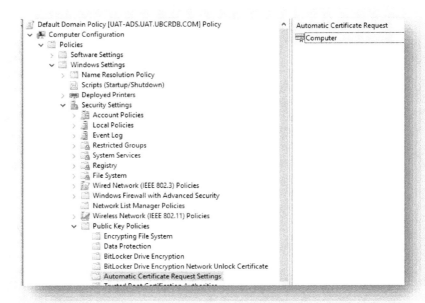

In the Certification Authority Manager, you will start to see a number of issued Computer (Machine) certificates to various servers within the domain.

STEP 5: CREATING AND DEPLOYING REMOTE DESKTOP PROTOCOL CERTIFICATES USING GROUP POLICY OBJECTS (GPO)

In the Server Manager, select the Tools Tab and click on the Certification Authority.

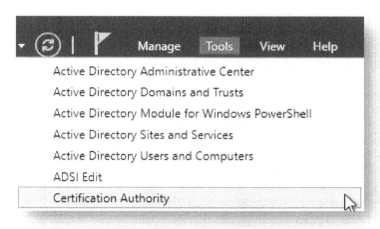

In the Certification Authority Manager, right-click on the Certificate Templates and select Manage.

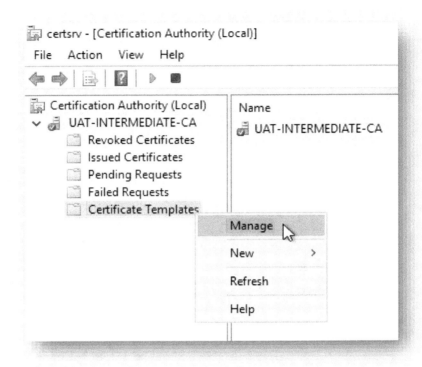

In the Certificate Templates Console, right-click on the Computer certificate and select the Duplicate Template option.

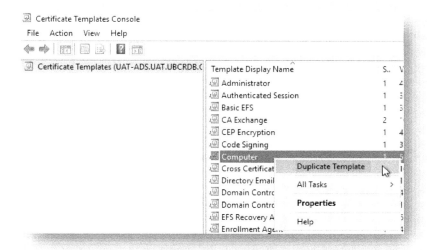

In the General Tab, put in the Template display name, Validity period, Renewal Period and make sure you check the "Publish certificate in Active Directory" box. Once done, click the Apply button.

 Microsoft

 Active Directory

Properties of New Template   ✕

Subject Name	Server	Issuance Requirements
Superseded Templates	Extensions	Security
Compatibility General Request Handling Cryptography Key Attestation

Template display name:

Remote Desktop Protocol Authentication (3389)

Template name:

RemoteDesktopProtocolAuthentication(3389)

Validity period: Renewal period:

10 years   ∨   6 weeks   ∨

☑ Publish certificate in Active Directory

   ☐ Do not automatically reenroll if a duplicate certificate exists in Active
      Directory

| | OK | Cancel | Apply | Help |

In the Extensions Tab under the "Extensions included in this template" section, click on the Application Policies and select Edit.

Properties of New Template ✕

Subject Name		Server		Issuance Requirements	
Compatibility	General	Request Handling	Cryptography		Key Attestation
	Superseded Templates		Extensions		Security

To modify an extension, select it, and then click Edit.

Extensions included in this template:

- Application Policies
- Basic Constraints
- Certificate Template Information
- Issuance Policies
- Key Usage

Edit...

Description of Application Policies:

Client Authentication
Server Authentication

OK	Cancel	Apply	Help

In the Application policies box, click on the Client Authentication and select the Remove button as we shall not need it in this template.

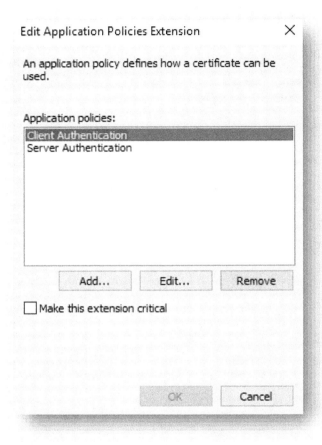

Click the Add button.

Edit Application Policies Extension   ✕

An application policy defines how a certificate can be used.

Application policies:

Server Authentication

Add...   Edit...   Remove

☐ Make this extension critical

OK   Cancel

In the "Add Application Policy" window click on the New button.

Type the Name of the Application Policy: Remote Desktop
Authentication (3389)
Set the Object identifier as 1.3.6.1.4.1.311.54.1.2, then click the OK
button.

You may also search for the "RemoteDesktopAuthentication" policy, if
it is already built in. Select it, then click the OK button.

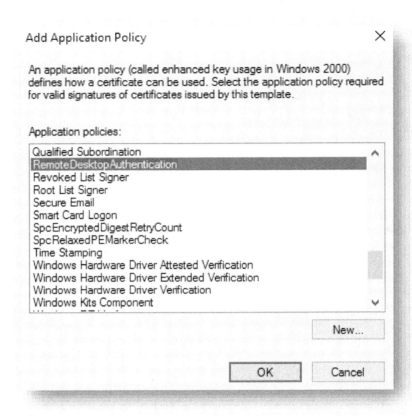

Back in the Application Policies Extension window, click the OK button.

Edit Application Policies Extension   ✕

An application policy defines how a certificate can be
used.

Application policies:

| RemoteDesktopAuthentication |
| Server Authentication |

[Add...]   [Edit...]   [Remove]

☐ Make this extension critical

[OK]   [Cancel]

Click on the Security Tab. In the Group or user names area, select the
Domain Computers. Edit the Permissions for Doma n Computers by
checking the "Read" and "Enroll" Check boxes. Click Apply to activate
the changes.

Properties of New Template   ✕

| Compatibility | General | Request Handling | Cryptography | Key Attestation |

| Subject Name | Server | Issuance Requirements |

| Superseded Templates | Extensions | Security |

Group or user names:

- 👥 Authenticated Users
- 👤 Robert Karamagi (rkaramagi@UAT.UBCRDB.COM)
- 👥 Domain Admins (UAT\Domain Admins)
- 👥 Domain Computers (UAT\Domain Computers)
- 👥 Enterprise Admins (UAT\Enterprise Admins)

     Add...   Remove

Permissions for Domain Computers   Allow   Deny

	Allow	Deny
Full Control	☐	☐
Read	☑	☐
Write	☐	☐
Enroll	☑	☐
Autoenroll	☐	☐

For special permissions or advanced settings, click Advanced.   Advanced

OK   Cancel   Apply   Help

160

 Microsoft

 Active Directory

Click the Cryptography Tab. Edit the Minimum key size to 4096 bits. Check the Microsoft RSA SChannel Cryptographic Provider checkbox, then click Apply to activate the settings.

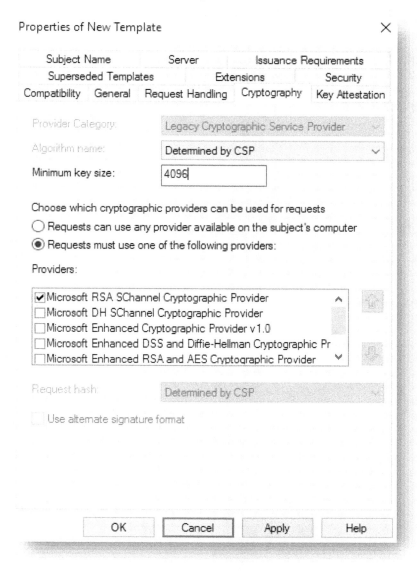

Properties of New Template ✕

Subject Name		Server		Issuance Requirements

	Superseded Templates		Extensions		Security

Compatibility	General	Request Handling	Cryptography	Key Attestation

Provider Category: Legacy Cryptographic Service Provider ⌄

Algorithm name: Determined by CSP ⌄

Minimum key size: 4096|

Choose which cryptographic providers can be used for requests

○ Requests can use any provider available on the subject's computer

◉ Requests must use one of the following providers:

Providers:

☑ Microsoft RSA SChannel Cryptographic Provider
☐ Microsoft DH SChannel Cryptographic Provider
☐ Microsoft Enhanced Cryptographic Provider v1.0
☐ Microsoft Enhanced DSS and Diffie-Hellman Cryptographic Pr
☐ Microsoft Enhanced RSA and AES Cryptographic Provider

Request hash: Determined by CSP ⌄

☐ Use alternate signature format

OK	Cancel	Apply	Help

Click on the Subject Name Tab. Select the "Build from this Active Directory information" option. In the Subject name format list, choose "Fully distinguished name". Check the "DNS name" checkbox under the heading "Include this information in alternate subject name".

Remote Desktop Protocol Authentication (3389) Prope...   ?   ✕

| Superseded Templates | Extensions | Security | Server |

| General | Compatibility | Request Handling | Cryptography | Key Attestation |

| Subject Name | Issuance Requirements |

○ Supply in the request

   ☐ Use subject information from existing certificates for autoenrollment renewal requests (*)

◉ Build from this Active Directory information

Select this option to enforce consistency among subject names and to simplify certificate administration.

Subject name format:

| Fully distinguished name ⌄ |

☐ Include e-mail name in subject name

Include this information in alternate subject name:

☐ E-mail name
☑ DNS name
☐ User principal name (UPN)
☐ Service principal name (SPN)

* Control is disabled due to compatibility settings.

| OK | Cancel | Apply | Help |

Go to the Group Policy Management and create a new Group Policy object.

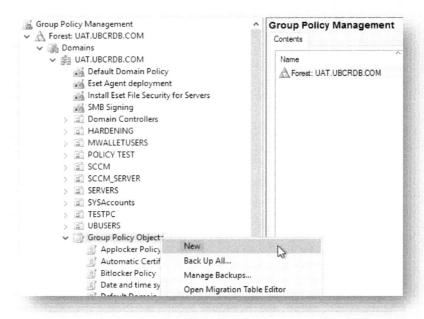

Give a name for the new GPO and click the OK button.

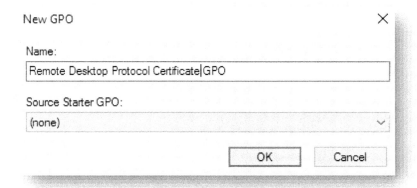

Right-click your newly created Group Policy Object (GPO) and select Edit.

Navigate to Computer configuration → Policies → Administrative Templates → Window Components → Remote Desktop Services → Remote Desktop Session Host → Security

Remote Desktop Protocol Certificate GPO [UAT-ADS.UAT.UBCRDB.COM] Policy
- Computer Configuration
  - Policies
    - Software Settings
    - Windows Settings
    - Administrative Templates: Policy definitions (ADMX files) retrieved from
      - Control Panel
      - Mozilla
      - Network
      - Printers
      - Server
      - Start Menu and Taskbar
      - System
      - Windows Components
        - ActiveX Installer Service
        - Add features to Windows 10
        - App Package Deployment
        - App Privacy

- Remote Desktop Services
  - RD Licensing
  - Remote Desktop Connection Client
  - Remote Desktop Session Host
    - Application Compatibility
    - Connections
    - Device and Resource Redirection
    - Licensing
    - Printer Redirection
    - Profiles
    - RD Connection Broker
    - Remote Session Environment
    - Security
    - Session Time Limits
    - Temporary folders

In the Security Settings, select "Server authentication certificate template" and click the Edit policy setting.

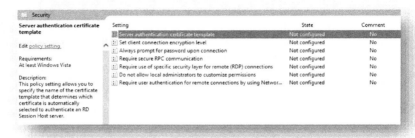

In the Server authentication certificate template select the "Enabled" radio button.
Under the Options, Place the exact same Template Name as set earlier:
i.e. "RemoteDesktopProtocolAuthentication(3389)"
Click Apply to activate the configuration.

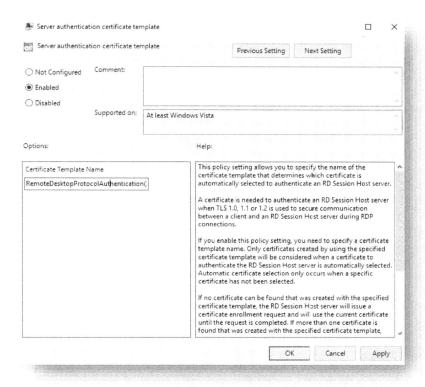

Again, in the Security settings, double-click the option "Require use of specific security layer for remote (RDP) connections" or click it once and select the Edit "policy setting" label.

Select the "Enabled" radio button and select the "SSL" security layer from the Options drop-down list. Click Apply to activate the changes.

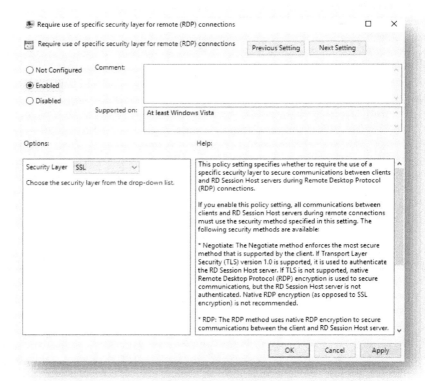

We will test the GPO by linking it to our "POLICY TEST" Organizational Unit Computer: "TTACE"

```
Active Directory Users and Computers [UAT        Name
  Saved Queries                                    TTACE
  UAT.UBCRDB.COM
      Builtin
      Computers
      Domain Controllers
      ForeignSecurityPrincipals
      HARDENING
      Managed Service Accounts
      MWALLETUSERS
      POLICY TEST
      SCCM
      SCCM_SERVER
      SERVERS
      SYSAccounts
      TESTPC
      UBUSERS
      Users
```

In the Group Policy Management menu, click the "POLICY TEST" organizational unit and select "Link an Existing GPO…"

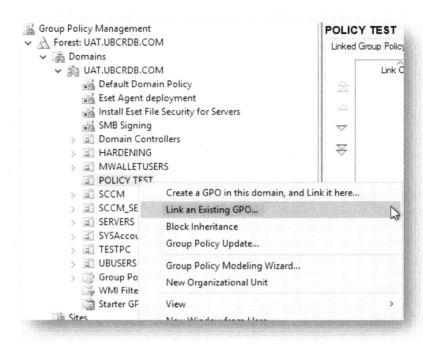

In the Group Policy objects list select the "Remote Desktop Protocol Certificate GPO" that we just created and click the OK button.

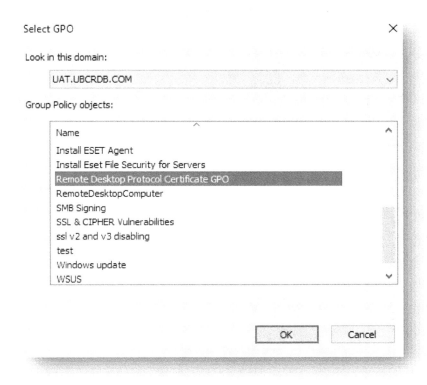

In the Group Policy Management, open the "POLICY TEST" Organization
Unit, right-click the Remote Desktop Protocol Certificate GPO and select
the Enforced option.

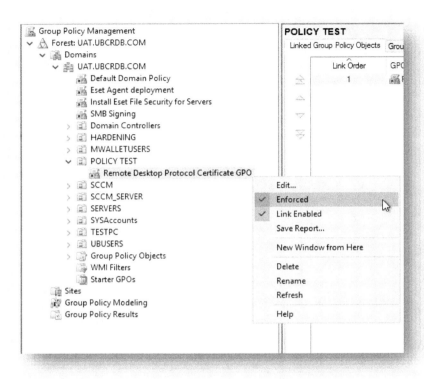

Run the gpupdate /force command with Administrator privileges on the Active Directory Domain Services server and client machine for the changes to take place immediately.

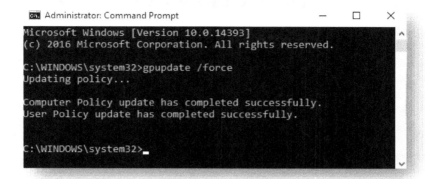

STEP 6: CONFIGURING THE CERTIFICATE THAT IS TO BE USED FOR REMOTE DESKTOP PROTOCOL USING A GROUP POLICY OBJECT (GPO)

Right-click the Remote Desktop Protocol Certificate GPO previously created and select Edit.

Navigate to Computer Configuration → Policies → Administrative Templates → Windows Components → Remote Desktop Services → Remote Desktop Client Host

Group Policy Management Editor

File   Action   View   Help

Remote Desktop Protocol Certificate GPO [UAT-ADS.UA ∧
∨ 🖳 Computer Configuration
  ∨ 🗂 Policies
    › 🗂 Software Settings
    › 🗂 Windows Settings
    ∨ 🗂 Administrative Templates: Policy definitions (
      › 🗂 Control Panel
      › 🗂 Mozilla
      › 🗂 Network
        🗂 Printers
        🗂 Server
        🗂 Start Menu and Taskbar
      › 🗂 System
      ∨ 🗂 Windows Components
          🗂 ActiveX Installer Service
          🗂 Add features to Windows 10
          🗂 App Package Deployment
          🗂 App Privacy
          🗂 App runtime
          🗂 Application Compatibility
          🗂 AutoPlay Policies

∨ 🗂 Remote Desktop Services
    🗂 RD Licensing
  › 🗂 Remote Desktop Connection Client
  › 🗂 Remote Desktop Session Host

Find the Intermediate Root Certification Authority Certificate from where you have stored it and open it.

Click on the Details Tab in the certificate then select and copy the sha1
thumbprint as shown below.

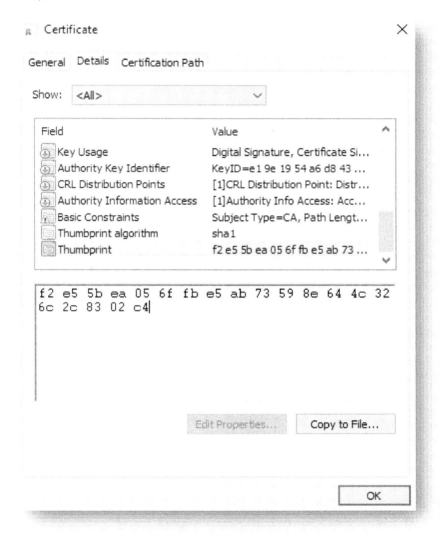

Correct SHA1 Thumbprint (✓):
F2E55BEA056FFBE5AB73598E644C326C2C8302C4

Wrong SHA1 Thumbprint (**X**): f2 e5 5b ea 05 6f fb e5 ab 73 59 8e 64 4c 32 6c 2c 83 02 c4

Edit the "Remote Desktop Connection Client" policy setting – "Specify SHA1 thumbprint of certificates representing trusted .rdp publishers"

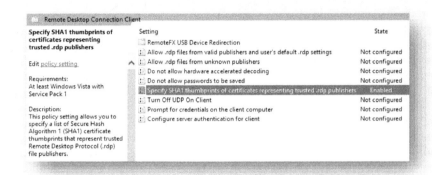

Select the "Enabled" radio button. Under the options, in the "Comma-separated list of SHA1 trusted certificate thumbprints", enter the SHA1 thumbprint taken from the Intermediate Certification Authority Certificate in the text box and click the Apply button for the changes to take effect.

Specify SHA1 thumbprints of certificates representing trusted .rdp publishers   ☐   ✕

Specify SHA1 thumbprints of certificates representing trusted .rdp publishers

[Previous Setting]   [Next Setting]

○ Not Configured   Comment:
● Enabled
○ Disabled

Supported on: At least Windows Vista with Service Pack 1

Options: Help:

Comma-separated list of SHA1 trusted certificate
thumbprints:

F2E55BEA056FFBE5AB73598E644C326C2C

This policy setting allows you to specify a list of Secure Hash
Algorithm 1 (SHA1) certificate thumbprints that represent trusted
Remote Desktop Protocol (.rdp) file publishers.

If you enable this policy setting, any certificate with an SHA1
thumbprint that matches a thumbprint on the list is trusted. If a
user tries to start an .rdp file that is signed by a trusted certificate,
the user does not receive any warning messages when they start
the file. To obtain the thumbprint, view the certificate details,
and then click the Thumbprint field.

If you disable or do not configure this policy setting, no
publisher is treated as a trusted .rdp publisher.

Notes:

You can define this policy setting in the Computer Configuration
node or in the User Configuration node. If you configure this
policy setting for the computer, the list of certificate thumbprints
trusted for a user is a combination of the list defined for the
computer and the list defined for the user.

[OK]   [Cancel]   [Apply]

STEP 7: CONFIGURING USER CERTIFICATES VIA A GROUP POLICY OBJECT (GPO)

We will start off by creating a TEST USERS organizational unit where will shall add a "Test User Group" which shall hold our test users. The test users in this organizational unit will be tested with the certificate policy. This method is a best practice whenever applying any type of new policy, instead of directly publishing it throughout the domain.

Open the Active Directory Users and Computers. Right-click the domain and select New → Organizational Unit.

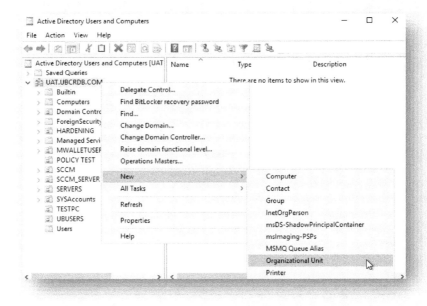

Give a name to the test organizational unit and click OK. We have called ours "TEST USERS".

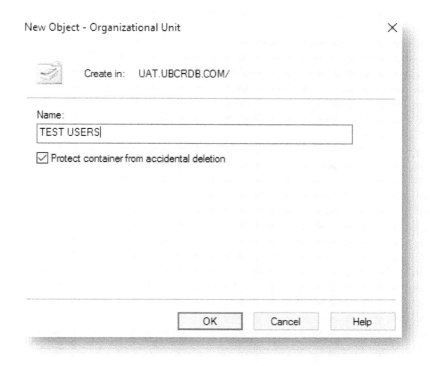

New Object - Organizational Unit   ✕

     Create in: UAT.UBCRDB.COM/

Name:

| TEST USERS| |

☑ Protect container from accidental deletion

         OK   Cancel   Help

Right-click the "TEST USERS" organizational unit and click New → Group

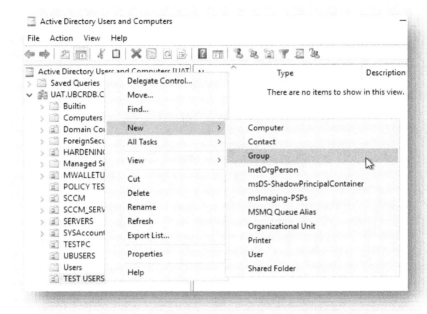

Type the Group name and click the OK button. We have called ours "Test User Group".

New Object - Group   ✕

    Create in: UAT.UBCRDB.COM/TEST USERS

Group name:

| Test User Group| |

Group name (pre-Windows 2000):

| Test User Group |

Group scope   Group type

○ Domain local   ● Security

● Global   ○ Distribution

○ Universal

                                    [OK   ]   [Cancel]

Right-click on the "TEST USERS" organizational unit again and select
New → User.

 Microsoft  Active Directory

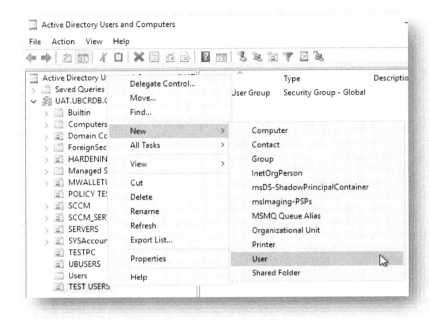

Provide the User details for the First name, Last name, User logon name then click the Next button.

New Object - User   ✕

Create in: UAT.UBCRDB.COM/TEST USERS

First name: | Roberto | Initials: | |

Last name: | Karamagi |

Full name: | Roberto Karamagi |

User logon name:

| rokaramagi | | @UAT.UBCRDB.COM   ∨ |

User logon name (pre-Windows 2000):

| UAT\ | | rokaramagi |

                                    | < Back | | Next > | | Cancel |

Enter the Password for the user and Confirm the password for the user
and click the Next button.

New Object - User   ✕

       Create in: UAT.UBCRDB.COM/TEST USERS

Password: •••••••

Confirm password: •••••••

☑ User must change password at next logon

☐ User cannot change password

☐ Password never expires

☐ Account is disabled

                              < Back   Next >   Cancel

Click the Finish button to finalize the user creation.

Right-click the newly created user and select the Properties.

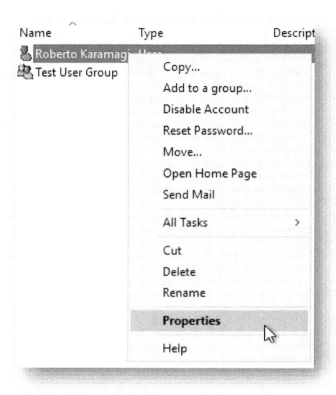

In the General Tab, add the Email for the User and click the Apply button to set the changes.

 Microsoft

 Active Directory

Roberto Karamagi Properties   ?   ✕

Member Of		Dial-in		Environment		Sessions
Remote control		Remote Desktop Services Profile			COM+
General	Address	Account	Profile	Telephones	Organization

Roberto Karamagi

First name: Roberto   Initials:

Last name: Karamagi

Display name: Roberto Karamagi

Description: Test User for Certificate Policy

Office: |

Telephone number: Other...

E-mail: roberto.karamagi@crdbbank.co.tz

Web page: Other...

| OK | Cancel | Apply | Help |

In the Member Of Tab, click the Add button.

Roberto Karamagi Properties ? ✕

Remote control		Remote Desktop Services Profile			COM+
General	Address	Account	Profile	Telephones	Organization
Member Of		Dial-in		Environment	Sessions

Member of:

Name	Active Directory Domain Services Folder
Domain Users	UAT.UBCRDB.COM/Users

Add...   Remove

Primary group: Domain Users

Set Primary Group   There is no need to change Primary group unless you have Macintosh clients or POSIX-compliant applications.

OK   Cancel   Apply   Help

Enter the "Test User Group" in the object names panel to add the User to that group.

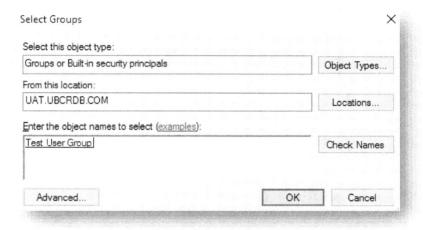

Once the "Test User Group" has appeared in the "Member of" Panel click the OK button.

Microsoft
 Active Directory

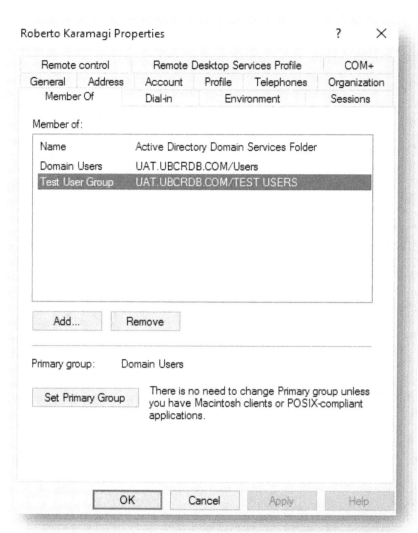

Roberto Karamagi Properties   ?   ✕

Remote control		Remote Desktop Services Profile			COM+
General	Address	Account	Profile	Telephones	Organization
Member Of		Dial-in		Environment	Sessions

Member of:

Name	Active Directory Domain Services Folder
Domain Users	UAT.UBCRDB.COM/Users
Test User Group	UAT.UBCRDB.COM/TEST USERS

[Add...]   [Remove]

Primary group: Domain Users

[Set Primary Group]   There is no need to change Primary group unless
you have Macintosh clients or POSIX-compliant
applications.

[OK]   [Cancel]   [Apply]   [Help]

Right-click the "Test User Group" and select the Properties.

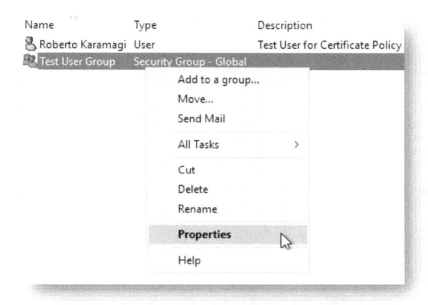

Notice that our user "Roberto Karamagi" has now appeared in the Members panel of the Test User Group.

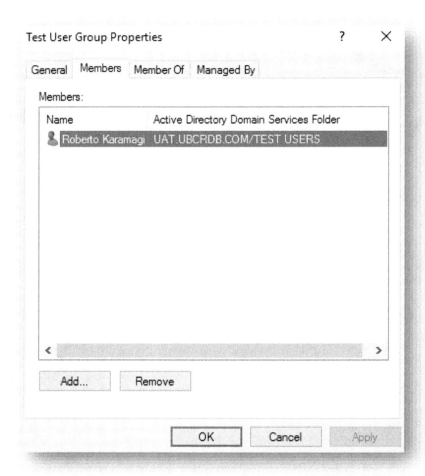

The respective User and Group in our "TEST USERS" organizational unit.

Name	Type	Description
Roberto Karamagi	User	Test User for Certificate Policy
Test User Group	Security Group - Global	

 Microsoft  Active Directory

In the Server Manager, click on Tools → Certification Authority

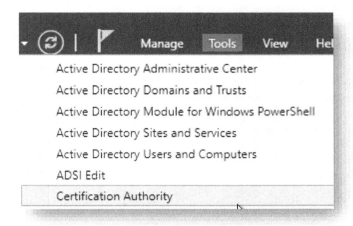

Right-click the Certificate Templates and select Manage.

In the Certificate Templates Console, right-click the User Template and select Duplicate Template.

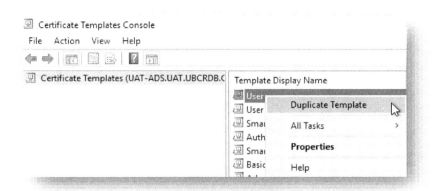

In the General Tab, enter your Template name in the "Template display name" text box. Ser the validity period and make sure that the "Publish certificate in Active Directory" checkbox is checked. Click the Apply button for the configuration to take effect.

Microsoft

 Active Directory

Properties of New Template   ✕

Subject Name		Server		Issuance Requirements
Superseded Templates			Extensions		Security
Compatibility	General	Request Handling	Cryptography	Key Attestation

Template display name:

User Certificate Test Template

Template name:

UserCertificateTestTemplate|

Validity period: Renewal period:

1 | years   ⌄   6 | weeks   ⌄

☑ Publish certificate in Active Directory

☐ Do not automatically reenroll if a duplicate certificate exists in Active
Directory

| OK | Cancel | Apply | Help |

Click on the "Request Handling" Tab. Check the box for "Allow private key to be exported". Select the radio button "Enroll subject without requiring any user input".

Properties of New Template　　　　　　　　　　✕

Subject Name		Server		Issuance Requirements
Superseded Templates		Extensions		Security
Compatibility	General	Request Handling	Cryptography	Key Attestation

Purpose: [Signature and encryption ⌄]

☐ Delete revoked or expired certificates (do not archive)

☑ Include symmetric algorithms allowed by the subject

☐ Archive subject's encryption private key

☑ Allow private key to be exported

☐ Renew with the same key (*)

☐ For automatic renewal of smart card certificates, use the existing key if a new key cannot be created (*)

Do the following when the subject is enrolled and when the private key associated with this certificate is used:

◉ Enroll subject without requiring any user input

◯ Prompt the user during enrollment

◯ Prompt the user during enrollment and require user input when the private key is used

* Control is disabled due to compatibility settings.

[OK]　[Cancel]　[Apply]　[Help]

Click on the "Cryptography" Tab. Set the minimum key size to 4096 or higher depending on your computing capabilities and click the Apply button.

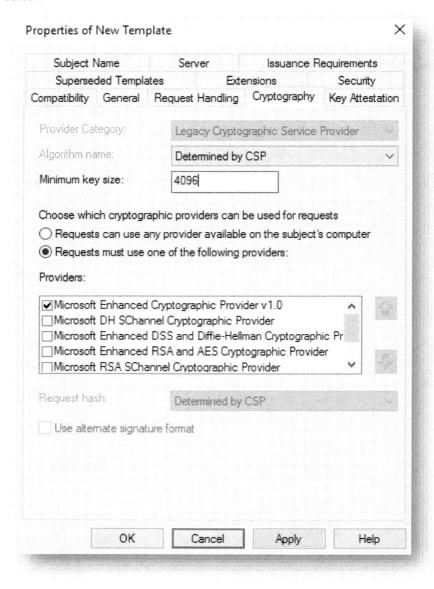

In the Security Tab, click the Add... button.

Properties of New Template   ✕

Subject Name		Server		Issuance Requirements
Compatibility	General	Request Handling	Cryptography	Key Attestation
Superseded Templates		Extensions		Security

Group or user names:

- 👥 Authenticated Users
- 👥 Domain Admins (UAT\Domain Admins)
- 👥 Domain Users (UAT\Domain Users)
- 👥 Enterprise Admins (UAT\Enterprise Admins)

[Add...]   [Remove]

Permissions for Domain Admins   Allow   Deny

Full Control	☐	☐
Read	☑	☐
Write	☑	☐
Enroll	☑	☐
Autoenroll	☐	☐

For special permissions or advanced settings, click Advanced.   [Advanced]

[OK]   [Cancel]   [Apply]   [Help]

Add the Test User Group previously created to the Security Template.

Select Users, Computers, Service Accounts, or Groups ✕

Select this object type:

| Users, Groups, or Built-in security principals | Object Types... |

From this location:

| UAT.UBCRDB.COM | Locations... |

Enter the object names to select (examples):

| Test User Group| | Check Names |

| Advanced... | | OK | Cancel |

In the "Permission for the Test User Group" panel check the Allow boxes: Read ,Enroll, Autoenroll. Click the Apply button to apply the changes.

Properties of New Template ✕

Subject Name		Server		Issuance Requirements	
Compatibility	General	Request Handling	Cryptography		Key Attestation
Superseded Templates		Extensions		Security	

Group or user names:

- 👥 Authenticated Users
- 👥 Domain Admins (UAT\Domain Admins)
- 👥 Domain Users (UAT\Domain Users)
- 👥 Enterprise Admins (UAT\Enterprise Admins)
- 👥 Test User Group (UAT\Test User Group)

[Add...] [Remove]

Permissions for Test User Group

	Allow	Deny
Full Control	☐	☐
Read	☑	☐
Write	☐	☐
Enroll	☑	☐
Autoenroll	☑	☐

For special permissions or advanced settings, click Advanced.

[Advanced]

[OK] [Cancel] [Apply] [Help]

Back in the Certification Authority Manager, right-click the Certificate Template, and select New → Certificate Template to Issue.

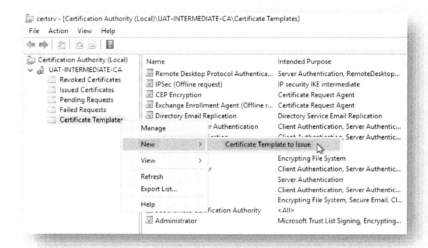

Select the User Certificate Test Template and click the OK button.

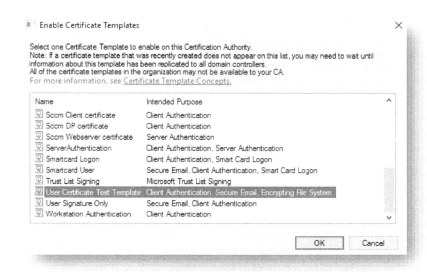

Open the Group Policy Manager. Right-click the Group Policy Objects and select New.

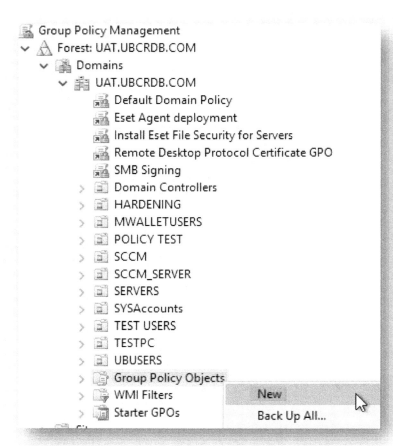

Enter the name of the New GPO and click the OK button.

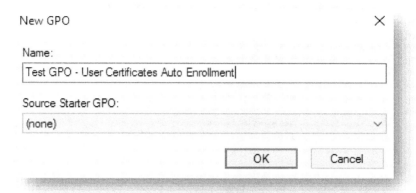

Right-click the newly created GPO and select Edit.

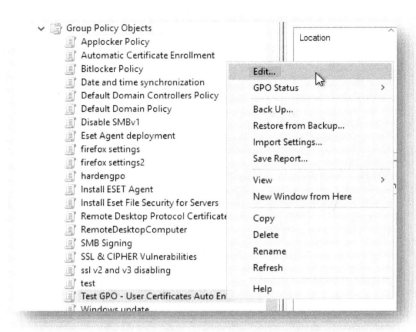

In the Group Policy Management Editor navigate to the User Configuration → Windows Settings → Security Settings → Public Key Policies.
Select the object "Certificate Services Client – Auto-Enrollment".

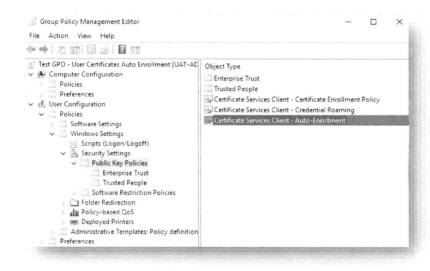

Set the configuration model to Enabled. Check the boxes for "Renew expired certificates, update pending certificates, and remove revoked certificates" and "Update certificates that use certificate templates". Click the Apply button to set the changes.

Certificate Services Client - Auto-Enrollment Properties   ?   ✕

Enrollment Policy Configuration

Enroll user and computer certificates automatically

Configuration Model: Enabled ▾

☑ Renew expired certificates, update pending certificates, and remove revoked certificates

☑ Update certificates that use certificate templates

Log expiry events and show expiry notifications when the percentage of remaining certificate lifetime is

[10 ▲▼]   %

Additional stores. Use "," to separate multiple stores. For example: "Store1, Store2, Store3"

[   ]

☐ Display user notifications for expiring certificates in user and machine MY store

[OK]   [Cancel]   [Apply]

Back in the Group Policy Management right-click the "TEST USERS" organizational unit and select Link an Existing GPO...

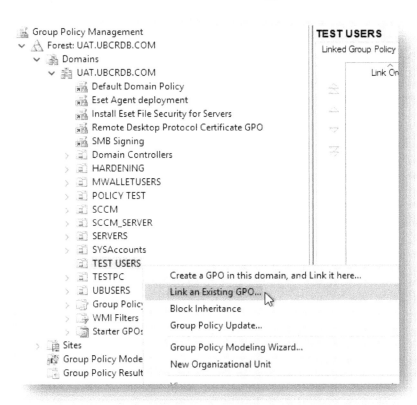

Select the GPO we created previously and click the OK button.

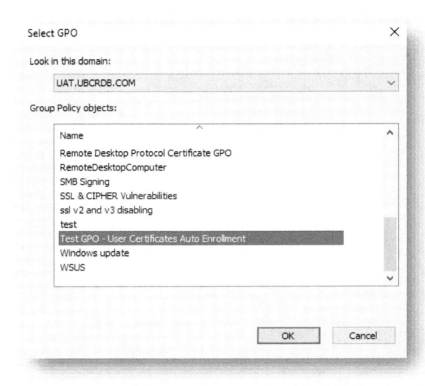

Right-click the visible GPO under the TEST USERS organizational unit and select the Enforced option.

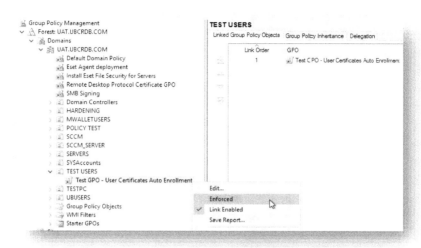

We shall navigate to the User Certificate Store when logged in as the user we have created previously to verify the certificate has automatically been pushed into the store.

Log into any server in the forest with the appropriate Test user credentials.

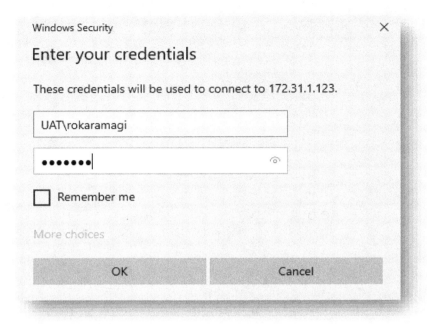

Open the Run (+ R), type "mmc" and click the OK button.

Click the Yes button to open the User Account Control.

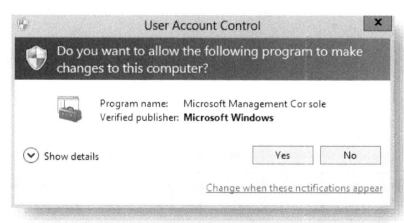

Click the File menu option and select Add/Remove Snap-in...

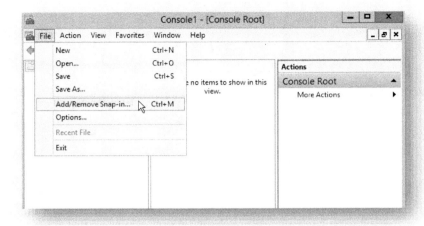

In the Add or Remove Snap-ins manager, click once on the "Certificates" in the available snap-ins panel and select the Add button.

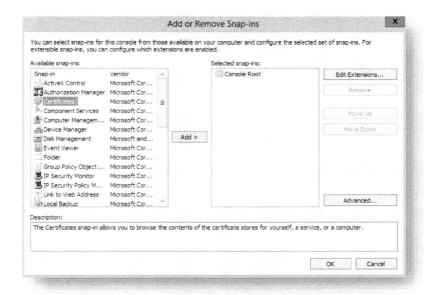

Once the "Certificate – Current User" snap in moves to the Selected snap-ins panel, click the OK button.

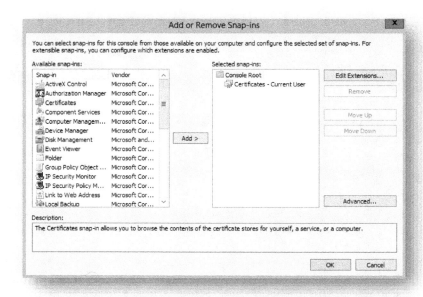

Select the "My user account" radio button and click on the Finish button.

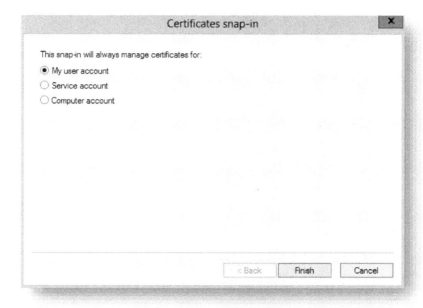

Navigate to the Personal Store and select the Certificates folder. The user certificate for the user shall be available.

Note: If the certificate is not available then open the command prompt and run the "gpupdate /force" command with Administrator privileges.

The certificate for our test user "Roberto Karamagi" is shown below:

Certificate [x]

General | Details | Certification Path

Certification path

UAT-ROOT-CA
  UAT-INTERMEDIATE-CA
    Roberto Karamagi

View Certificate

Certificate status:

This certificate is OK.

Learn more about certification paths

OK